Solkattu Manual

Solkattu Manual

AN INTRODUCTION TO THE RHYTHMIC LANGUAGE OF SOUTH INDIAN MUSIC

David P. Nelson

WESLEYAN UNIVERSITY PRESS Middletown, Connecticut

Published by Wesleyan University Press,
Middletown, CT 06459
www.wesleyan.edu/wespress

ISBN: 978-0-8195-7523-4

Wesleyan University Press is a member of the
Green Press Initiative. The paper used in this book
meets their minimum requirement for recycled paper.

Printed in the United States of America
5 4 3 2

The Library of Congress has catalogued the original printing
as follows:

Nelson, David P.
Solkattu manual : an introduction to the rhythmic language
of South Indian music / David P. Nelson.
p. cm.
ISBN 978-0-8195-6871-7 (pbk. : alk. paper)
1. Tala. 2. Carnatic music—Instruction and study. I. Title.
MT42.N34 2008
780.954'8—dc22 2008007654

CONTENTS

Video with exercises for parts 1–3 can be found at www.wesleyan.edu/wespress/solkattu.

ACKNOWLEDGMENTS

This project would never have been possible without the efforts of T. Ranganathan and T. Viswanathan, who dedicated their careers to teaching Karnatak music in the United States. Their profundity as artists and teachers has been a lifelong source of inspiration to me. I am also grateful to my predecessor at Wesleyan, Ramnad V. Raghavan, for his support and continuing friendship.

I wrote this book during a sabbatical semester from Wesleyan University, for whose support I am grateful. I also thank Suzanna Tamminen and her staff at Wesleyan University Press for their well-organized help and good cheer.

Shortly after I began teaching at Wesleyan, my dissertation advisor and mentor Jon Barlow stopped me in the music department lobby one day and asked, "How would you convince a liberal arts music program that they should teach solkattu?" That question echoed in my mind for five years until I wrote this book. Thank you, Jon, for that and for so much more.

Allynn Wilkinson, Wesleyan's Digitization specialist and a valued colleague and friend, was invaluable in putting together the video portion of this book. I could never have done it without her expertise, patience, and humor. Mariah Klaneski, Allynn's choice as videographer and video editor, was patient with me and attentive to the material at every stage.

Ruby Ross, Aaron Paige, Dennis Chan, and Geoffrey Brown came together from distant places and performed beautifully for the video. My sincere thanks to all of them for their talent, hard work, and spirit. Fugan Dineen, my incomparable teaching assistant for the past four years, took meticulous notes during my solkattu classes and organized them so that I could see what we had done.

Jamey Haddad, Tim Eriksen, and Rory Stuart all made extremely helpful comments along the way. I thank them all, as well as Richard Winslow and David Reck for their insight and support.

For the notation, I used Solkattu Workshop, a program developed by Greg Jalbert at imaja.com. I appreciate Greg's efforts in helping me get the most out of the software. For the text, I used UniTms, a Unicode transliteration font developed by Lloyd Anderson at Ecological Linguistics.

My heartfelt thanks to my friend and translator Christian Scheuber, for his sharp eyes in identifying typos and unclear passages in the first edition.

Finally, but by no means least, my love and thanks to my wife Kim, whose unflagging mental, physical and spiritual support have made this and so many other projects worth doing.

Solkattu Manual

INTRODUCTION

WHAT IS SOLKAṬṬU?

India's classical music entered American and European popular culture in the late 1950s and early 1960s through performances of *Hindustani* (North Indian classical) music by sitarist Ravi Shankar and sarodist Ali Akbar Khan. These great musicians performed with *tabla* players who dazzled American and European audiences by alternately playing and vocalizing intricate percussion patterns during their solo passages. Musicians and non-musicians alike were amazed that these drummers could voice such precise patterns at blazing speed, and play them with equal precision on their drums. And they appeared to be enjoying themselves enormously.

Indian music enjoyed a surge of popularity in the West during this period, and *Karnatak* (South Indian classical) musicians joined their northern cousins at festivals and on concert tours. It became clear that spoken rhythm patterns were not just North Indian; apparently *all* Indian drummers could speak what they played.

It was not long before European and American musicians and students began to seek out teachers from whom they could learn the sophisticated rhythms that were delighting them in the concerts. And soon colleges and universities in the West were incorporating "world music" into their curricula, bringing visiting artists from India, Africa, and Indonesia to teach their music.

For many young musicians, looking beyond Europe and America for musical information and inspiration meant going to Asia and Africa for direct contact with the source. As one of these musical pilgrims, I traveled to Madurai, in the heart of Tamil Nadu, India, during a year-abroad program in 1970 under the aegis of the Great Lakes Colleges Association. There I began my study of the *mrdangam*, South Indian music's principal percussion instrument. In my very first lesson under the legendary court musician and teacher C. S. Sankarasivam, I was introduced to the rhythm language, called *solkaṭṭu*, that is the subject of this book.

The Tamil word solkaṭṭu means "words bound together," which is an elegant definition. The "words" are more or less percussive-sounding single syllables, nearly all of which begin with consonants. They are "bound together" on two levels: first, into combinations that comprise phrases, for example *ta ka di mi*. The phrases are then combined into larger patterns and designs bound together by meters, called *tāḷa*. These cyclic meters are counted by recurring sets of hand gestures: claps, waves, and finger counts. Speaking such patterns while counting a tāḷa with the hands is solkaṭṭu.

While a detailed account of tāḷa is not necessary for this introduction to solkaṭṭu, it will be helpful to know what a tāḷa is (and is not). I have been using the word *meter* as an English equivalent in this introduction. In a broad sense, meter is a useful translation for tāḷa; each is cyclic and regular, and each can exist within a range of tempi. But there are two differences. First, a tāḷa lacks the internal accent structure that characterizes meters in Western music. For example, 3/4 meter carries the following accent structure:

strong weak weak *strong* weak weak

A corresponding three-beat tāḷa, *tiśra jāti ēka tāḷa*, is counted with the palm and fingers of one hand against the other:

clap, pinky finger, ring finger, *clap*, pinky finger, ring finger

But there is no implied accent, even on the clapped first beat. Rhythmic accents in Karnatak music are generated by musical phrases and the processes applied to them. The first lessons in this book will demonstrate this point.

Next, a tāḷa can be much longer than any Western meter. Many of the tāḷas in the scheme of thirty-five described below are quite long; the longest cycle is twenty-nine beats. At the slow end of the possible range of tempi, about thirty beats per minute, one cycle of this tāḷa takes nearly a minute, which is an extremely long time by the standards of Western music.

Uses of Solkaṭṭu in South Indian Music

The patterns and designs of any Karnatak music that makes use of tāḷa can be expressed in solkaṭṭu. In other words, whether a passage is sung, played, danced, or drummed in a meter, its underlying rhythmic pattern can be spoken in syllables along with the particular tāḷa's hand gestures. Let us look at three ways solkaṭṭu is used in Karnatak music: in drumming; in *bharata nāṭyam*, or classical dance; and as a compositional and analytic tool for singers and melodic instrumentalists.

SOLKAṬṬU IN KARNATAK DRUMMING

As I said earlier, I was introduced to solkaṭṭu in my first mrdangam lesson. Each stroke on the drum had a corresponding spoken syllable; the first four were *ta*, *di*, *tom*, and *nam*. The first lessons progressed by inserting other syllables among these four in order to build longer patterns bounded by the original four syllables:

ta - ki ṭa
di - ki ṭa
tom - ki ṭa
nam - ki ṭa, then

ta - ki ṭa ta ka
di - ki ṭa ta ka
tom - ki ṭa ta ka
nam - ki ṭa ta ka, and so on

My teacher taught each new pattern first with the syllables, his hands clapping a simple, regular beat. Once I understood the spoken pattern, he showed me the corresponding strokes on the mrdangam. After the beginning exercises, every pattern was in a particular tāḷa. Although there was never a one-to-one correspondence of syllable with stroke, over time the relationship between the two became clear.

The arrangement of strokes and the arrangement of syllables are parallel: the former follows a logic of the hand, while the latter follows a logic of spoken sound. In other words, played patterns are designed so that the fingers can execute them deftly. Spoken patterns are designed so that they can be voiced with equal dexterity. Throughout my training, I learned literally everything in two forms, spoken and played.

All of the Karnatak percussion instruments are taught in this manner. Some drummers become so expert in reciting solkaṭṭu that they perform it in their concerts, either during their solos, like the tabla players that amazed us in the early days, or as secondary percussionists in a performance ensemble. Solkaṭṭu performed in a concert setting is called *konakkol*.

SOLKAṬṬU IN BHARATA NĀṬYAM

South India's classical dance, bharata nāṭyam, uses solkaṭṭu in several different ways to create a rich rhythmic texture. First, dancers learn their movement patterns, called *aḍavu*, using spoken patterns in very much the same way as drummers, though with somewhat different sets of syllables. A particular phrase, spoken with the tāḷa, indicates a corresponding set of foot and hand movements.

These movement patterns are arranged into set compositions, called *jati* and *tīrmanam*, that are accompanied by an ensemble of musicians. The ensemble includes a *naṭṭuvanar*, or dance master, who accompanies some of the jati and tīrmanam by speaking corresponding compositions in solkaṭṭu while playing the aḍavu pattern on a set of hand cymbals. The naṭṭuvanar uses yet another set of syllables, similar to those used by drummers. The solkaṭṭu composition performed by the dance master often creates rhythmic tension with the aḍavu pattern, though the two begin and end together.

The dance ensemble also includes a singer and a mrdangam player. If we keep in mind that any pattern sung or played in a tāḷa can be represented by solkaṭṭu, a bharata nāṭyam tīrmanam comprises five such layers: the song text, the naṭṭuvanar's voice and cymbal patterns, the dancer's footwork, and the mrdangam strokes.

SOLKAṬṬU IN MELODIC COMPOSITION AND ANALYSIS

Singers and instrumental players of Karnatak music borrow rhythmic designs from drummers for use in their *svara kalpana* improvisation. This kind of improvisation uses the Indian solfege syllables *sa ri ga ma pa da ni* to create melodic passages that resolve at a specific point within a particular song. Many musicians end such improvised passages with rhythmic designs that they have learned and practiced ahead of time. These designs, called *mōrā* and *kōrvai*, are worked out using solkaṭṭu before their melodies are set.

In addition, a melodic musician who finds any musical passage rhythmically challenging is likely to work it out in rhythmic syllables before attempting to sing or play it. The vocabulary of syllables and patterns that melodic musicians use is not as rich or detailed as those used by drummers and dance masters, but this use of solkaṭṭu has perhaps the broadest implications. Musicians who use solkaṭṭu to solve problematic passages take this expressive rhythmic language out of the realm of drum and dance syllables and into the world of general rhythmic analysis and training.

Solkaṭṭu, then, pervades every aspect of metered Karnatak music, which is among the most rhythmically sophisticated of the world's music systems. It is also a powerful tool for developing a strong sense of well-organized rhythm in nearly any form of music, as the rest of this book will demonstrate.

Why Study Solkaṭṭu?

It may be surprising to find out that such a valuable method for rhythm training is not taught on its own in India. Drummers, dancers, and melodic musicians learn whatever aspects of solkaṭṭu are appropriate for their respective disciplines, and musicians intuitively adapt it for their own analytic uses. There is really no need for a separate course in solkaṭṭu.

But in the West, many musicians and composers have become interested in the rhythmic intricacy of Indian music. Most of these musicians do not have the time or inclination to take up a full study of Indian music or dance. For them, a separate course in solkaṭṭu is an ideal way to learn the rhythms of Indian music without having to take on a new musical instrument or technique. In addition, many teachers of basic musicianship have become interested in the elegance and effectiveness of solkaṭṭu as a method for training in fundamental rhythmic skills. This interest is largely due to three of solkaṭṭu's most important attributes: the *physical confidence* it develops, its *portability*, and its *inherent musicality*.

PHYSICAL CONFIDENCE

Solkaṭṭu binds spoken material together within the metric context called tāḷa, which is counted by recurrent patterns of hand gestures. Since the same person is speaking patterns and counting tāḷa, this binding together is a somatic, kinesthetic experience; it all happens within the same body. The relationship between the phrases and the tāḷa is either accurate or not: if so, there is a feeling of confidence; if not, the musician knows immediately that something is awry and can move to correct it. Over time, one learns to trust this bodily knowledge. As the coordination of voice and hand becomes a matter of muscle memory, musicians find that they are able to learn challenging rhythms more and more quickly.

PORTABILITY

Solkaṭṭu requires no instrument for practice or performance. One can practice anywhere—in one's room, on a train, in line at the bank—while doing anything—walking, standing, sitting, or lying down. Obviously, the tāḷa gestures and syllables must be performed without disturbing others or drawing unnecessary attention to the practicer. But this portability makes it possible to call a pattern or exercise to mind virtually anywhere. My solkaṭṭu course is usually taught in the spring, and I often see students walking along on warm April days, apparently talking to themselves. A closer look often reveals the telltale signs of impromptu solkaṭṭu practice: the mouth moving slightly, a hand beating time on the thigh, and a faraway look in the eyes.

INHERENT MUSICALITY

Solkaṭṭu always includes spoken phrases within a tāḷa; there is never a situation in which something happens in a tāḷa that cannot be spoken by a musical phrase. Consider the usual method of counting sixteenth notes in 4/4 time:

one e and a *two* e and a *three* e and a *four* e and a

Here numbers demonstrate the rhythm; there is no specific musical content involved. This may be called abstract, or *meter*-centered, counting.

The same number of syllables may be counted within the same number of beats in a four-beat tāḷa, as follows. Touch the palm and fingers of one hand against the other:

clap, pinky, ring, middle

Instead of counting in numbers, a Karnatak musician uses syllables, four for each beat, as follows:

clap	pinky	ring	middle
ta ka di mi	*ta ka di mi*	*ta ka di mi*	*ta ka di mi*

This is an example of a *phrase*-centered approach to counting. Karnatak musicians virtually never count in numbers, even when marking rests, but in syllables. The inherent musicality of using phrases instead of numbers for counting makes solkaṭṭu immediately approachable for students. Previously exotic-sounding syllables and phrases quickly take on concrete musical meaning. Rhythm training, which can be dry and abstract, is suddenly accessible and fun.

Sources of Syllables and Tāḷas

Information about solkaṭṭu syllables and tāḷas comes from two intertwined sources: the unwritten legacy passed along from teacher to student through at least two millennia of Indian music, including more than ten thousand Karnatak songs, and the treatises written by musicologists and music theoreticians during the same period. These two sources are not always easily separated. A treatise is usually based on the performance practice of a given period and often represents an attempt to codify it. To the extent that it succeeds, it may in turn actually *influence* performance practice.

SYLLABLES

Our main source regarding the syllables is the teaching lineage itself, specifically that of the mrdangam and other percussion instruments. Spoken syllables, including the first four mentioned above, *ta, di, tom*, and *nam*, are the beginning of any mrdangam student's training. They also appear in the *Nāṭyaśāstra* (ca. 200 BCE–200 CE) and other treatises.

Indian writers on music have largely ignored the subject of drumming, and non-Indian writers on Indian drumming have, until recently, reduced the place of spoken rhythmic syllables to the role of "drum syllables," mnemonic devices meant to imitate the sounds produced on the mrdangam, *tavil*, and other percussion instruments. But as Douglass Fugan Dineen pointed out in his 2005 M.A. thesis from Wesleyan University ("At Home and Abroad: An Investigation of Solkaṭṭu in Karnatak and Non-Karnatak Contexts"), the Karnatak tradition has never limited the use of syllables to drumming. *All* Karnatak musicians and dancers use them.

The vocabulary of syllables in this text comes from my study of the mrdangam under T. Ranganathan (1925–1987), himself a disciple of Palani Sri M. Subramania Pillai (1908–1962). Sri Ranganathan's teaching career in the United States spanned more than twenty years at Wesleyan University and the California Institute of the Arts. I was his student at both schools and served as his teaching apprentice during my residency as a Ph.D. candidate at Wesleyan from 1980 to 1983. It was at these two institutions that Ranganathan first taught solkaṭṭu as a subject separate from drumming. My vocabulary of syllables has also been influenced by more than six years of teaching solkaṭṭu at Wesleyan.

TĀḶAS

Our sources regarding tāḷas are more convoluted. The biggest difficulty in tracing the practical history of tāḷa is the lack of written music; Indian music has always been an oral tradition. The earliest writings *about* Indian music, beginning with the Nāṭyaśāstra, describe tāḷas as sets of hand gestures. From the thirteenth century on, tāḷas seem to have been cyclic. The best sources from the history of performance practice are the songs that form the repertoire of Karnatak music and the pedagogical exercises teachers use to prepare students to learn them. We can gather from these that tāḷas have been used as regular, cyclic meters since at least the sixteenth century.

For the last hundred years or so, conventional wisdom has assumed the existence of thirty-five tāḷas, although no one seems to know who originated them. A group of seven tāḷa structures (sets of hand gestures) is typically presented as the *suladi sapta tāḷas*. Each of these includes at least one *laghu*, a tāḷa segment made up of a clap and finger counts. By allowing five different durations for the laghu (four, three, seven, five, and nine beats, using the traditional order), each of these seven can have five possible beat totals, for a total of thirty-five. According to the noted music scholar N. Ramanathan (personal communication, 2006), the thirty-five-tāḷa scheme first appeared in "Oriental Music in Western Notation," a journal written by A. M. Chinnaswamy Mudaliar in 1893. Since that time a table of thirty-five tāḷas may be seen in nearly every book on South Indian music and need not be reproduced in this introductory text.

The main body of material here is in the eight-beat cycle ādi tāḷa, which occurs among the thirty-five as *caturaśra jāti tripuṭa tāḷa*. The name *ādi* (Sanskrit: ancient, primordial) suggests that this meter has importance beyond its existence as one among five possibilities for tripuṭa tāḷa, one of the suladi sapta tāḷas mentioned above. Indeed, more than 80 percent of the songs in the Karnatak music repertoire are composed in this tāḷa, and the bulk of any mrdangam student's training is in this dominant meter.

While the thirty-five-tāḷa scheme is preeminent in writings on Karnatak music, modern performance practice tells a different story. Ādi tāḷa is the only one of the four most commonly performed tāḷas that is represented among the thirty-five. The others, *rūpaka* (three beats), *miśra cāpu* (seven beats), and *khaṇḍa cāpu* (five beats), are counted by means of simple claps and waves and omit the laghu (clap plus finger counts) that makes the thirty-five-tāḷa scheme possible. The three principal composers of Karnatak music, Tyagaraja (1767–1847), Muttuswami Diksitar (1775–1835), and Syama Sastri (1762–1827), composed their songs mainly in these four meters; they used only a few tāḷas out of the thirty-five. But as I said above, musicological writings can influence performance practice, and this has been the case with the thirty-five-tāḷa scheme. Some teachers use them for composing voice and instrumental exercises, and many musicians use them for composing the brief, challenging pieces known as *pallavi*. I have used the simplest tāḷa in the scheme, *ēka*, which consists of a solitary laghu, in its five possible values to compose exercises for this book.

Solkaṭṭu, then, is a real-time, *embodied* rhythmic notation that can be a powerful and enjoyable tool in rhythm training. The lessons in this book begin with fundamental exercises designed to build rhythmic skills in the simplest Karnatak tāḷa. The next lessons develop two core concepts of Karnatak rhythm, flow and design, and add advanced exercises in three more tāḷas. The largest section, entirely in ādi tāḷa, generates a range of possible percussion solo and ensemble pieces in the modern Karnatak idiom. A glossary and pronunciation guide accompanies each section. The material in this book will develop and strengthen one's sense of rhythm in energetic and fascinating ways while providing a personal, palpable appreciation of the Indian musicians whose command of musical time has mesmerized and delighted us for the last half-century.

THE STRUCTURE OF THE LESSONS

These lessons are designed to build a practical understanding of rhythm in South Indian music from the ground up and assume no previous exposure to Karnatak music. Because solkaṭṭu is not taught as a separate subject in India, there is no pedagogical paradigm to guide a beginner. I have spent two decades refining my own teaching method, however, which is aimed at American musicians and college students. What follows is a brief outline of my method as presented in this book.

Part I: Tiśra Jāti Ēka Tāḷa

The first series of lessons is in the deceptively simple three-beat cycle tiśra jāti ēka tāḷa, the shortest in the thirty-five-tāḷa scheme. A three-syllable pattern introduces a fundamental process, the *trikāla* (three speeds), and seven related exercises.

The second series of lessons in tiśra jāti ēka tāḷa combines patterns from the first series into phrases. These phrases are arranged into a rudimentary rhythmic composition, ending with a simple mōrā (ending design), along with an explanation of the mōrā form. Two core concepts, flow (*sarvalaghu*) and design (*kaṇakku*), are introduced.

Mōrā series 1 uses the mōrā that ended the second series composition to develop a further series of six mōrās, designed to be performed in sequence. This series includes allowable exceptions to the mōrā form, as defined in the previous section.

Mōrā series 2 develops another series of mōrās using a different principle of expansion.

Part II: Exercise Mōrās

This series of thirteen mōrās in four tāḷas is designed to develop two areas of strength. First, it introduces persistent offbeat accents and includes practice strategies for mastering them. Second, since the mōrās themselves are substantially more complex than those in the previous section, it develops a more highly developed sense of form and rhythmic design.

Part III: Ādi Tāḷa Lessons

The main section of this book follows a typical mrdangam student's training in Karnatak music's predominant tāḷa. These lessons take the form of a *tani āvartanam*, the percussion solo included in every concert. They begin with a series of mōrās that introduces the notion of the *compound* mōrā. Subsequent lessons include other types of Karnatak rhythmic design, such as *kōrvai* and *koraippu*, as well as sections that shift the internal pulse of each beat from four to three and five. The ādi tāḷa lessons conclude with a stylized ending section characteristic of the tani āvartanam.

Conclusion: Putting It All Together

The concluding section provides a written account of three pieces made from the ādi tāḷa lessons. These pieces, included on the accompanying video, are examples of how the student might arrange the material for his or her own needs.

Video Examples and Notation

Throughout the text are links to the 150 examples found on the accompanying video at www.wesleyan.edu/wespress/solkattu. These are indicated by numeric codes in bold type, such as (**01-001**). The two-digit prefix refers to the chapter number, while the three-digit number refers to the example itself. The bold letter "**N**" following one of these numbers indicates that there is also notation for it.

I use minimal notation in my courses, mainly as a jog to the memory. For the sake of convenience I have provided notation, in tāḷa and syllables, for eighty-eight of the exercises and patterns in this book. The notation should be used as a reference, not as a primary means of learning the material. Once a piece has been memorized, the notation will have served its purpose.

Some readers will be tempted to represent material in this book in staff notation. While I will not say it is wrong to do this, I find it at best culturally dissonant and at worst misleading. In any case, the syllable/tāḷa notation in this book, supported by exhaustive video examples, should make it unnecessary.

HOW TO USE THIS BOOK

This book may be used in several ways. An interested individual could certainly use it for self-training, as could a group of musicians. I have successfully used this method with classes of up to twenty students. Here are some suggestions, section by section. Perhaps the most important suggestion is to enjoy the process. Solkaṭṭu should be fun!

Part I: Tiśra Jāti Ēka Tāḷa

CHAPTER 1: LESSONS, FIRST SERIES

The entire first section is designed for beginners, not just in Indian rhythm studies but in *general* rhythm studies. I have used it in entry-level music courses with great success. The exercises are supported by clear, detailed notation and video examples. These are truly fundamental lessons; they should be taught, practiced, and mastered with great care. Every subsequent lesson is built on the foundation established by these lessons. Once they have been mastered using the original three-note phrase, they should be repeated with each of the substitute phrases, until any of them can be performed on demand.

CHAPTERS 2–4: LESSONS, SECOND SERIES, AND MŌRĀ SERIES 1 AND 2

Each student should learn to perform both series according to the instructions. Again, the notation and video support will be extremely helpful. Students should learn to perform this material without looking at the notation. Remember that Karnatak music is an *oral* tradition.

Once each student has mastered every mōrā, they can be performed in turn by a group of musicians. The group can recite the main body of the composition, using the mōrās as small solos for individual students.

Part II: Exercise Mōrās

CHAPTER 5

These mōrās should be learned and mastered one at a time. I use an exercise mōrā at the beginning of each class session as a kind of tune-up; first the group performs it together, then each student performs it in turn. Once everybody has a good command of a particular exercise mōrā, we go on to the next one. I recommend doing all four versions of exercise mōrā 1 before going on to the others. Do only the mōrās that can be handled comfortably; there is no reason to do them all. On the other hand, if the group breezes through them, feel free to make up variations.

Part III: Ādi Tāḷa Lessons

CHAPTERS 6–12

I strongly recommend that all members of the class or group work through all of the versions and variations of each mōrā, kōrvai, and koraippu pattern in this part of the book. This will reinforce the important point that the material is extremely flexible and can appear in any of the forms presented.

Naturally, when it comes to performing the full composition, parts and variations will be assigned and practiced, and the performance order will be set. But this should be delayed as long as possible. In addition to the video examples of each lesson, chapter 12, "Putting It All Together," provides three examples of performance pieces for groups of varying sizes. Feel free to experiment.

Pronunciation

Two different types of pronunciation guide are used in this book. The first concerns Sanskrit and Tamil words; the second, the solkaṭṭu syllables. This pronunciation guide applies to the former—pronunciation of the syllables will be handled on a case-by-case basis throughout the text:

vowels may be short—*a (opera, cinema), e (pet), i (tip), o (porch), u (put)*—or long—*ā (blah), ē (say), ī (tee), ō (blow), ū (tool)*

consonants *t* and *d* are *dental*, pronounced with the tongue flat against the top teeth

consonants with dots underneath, *ḍ, ṭ, ḷ, ṇ*, are *retroflex*, pronounced with the tip of the tongue curled against the roof of the mouth, as if a liquid "r" preceded them: *bird, curt, snarling, corn*

ś sounds like *flash*, *s* sounds like *dust*, not *music*

r is like the single Spanish *r*, in which the tongue bounces once off the roof of the mouth, not like the liquid American *row*

j and *g* sound like *jog*

c sounds like *church*

Accents in Sanskrit and Tamil words are functions of long and short syllables. If all the vowels in a word are short, the syllables are pronounced with equal weight, for example *sol-kaṭ-ṭu*, not *SOL-kaṭ-ṭu* or *sol-KAṬ-ṭu*. A long vowel in a word generates an accent, for example *TĀ-ḷa, san-KĪR-ṇa*. Most of the non-English words in this text can be sounded out using this scheme. One exception is the Sanskrit *caturaśra*, which most Tamil-speaking Karnatak musicians pronounce as *cha-TOOSH-ra* or *cha-TOOS-ra*. The following glossary includes approximate pronunciations and definitions for the non-English terms used in this introduction.

GLOSSARY

aḍavu (ah-dah-voo): A basic movement pattern in bharata nāṭyam.

ādi tāḷa (AH-dee TAH-la): The predominant tāḷa in Karnatak music. Its eight beats are counted with a four-beat laghu and two *drutams* (clap and wave).

bharata nāṭyam (ba-ra-ta NOT-yum): South India's classical dance.

caturaśra jāti (cha-TOOSH-ra JAH-tee): The family of four-beat rhythms. Also, when referring to the *laghu*, four beats.

ēka tāḷa (ACHE-a TAH-la): A tāḷa made up of a single clap and finger counts (laghu).

Hindustani (hin-du-STAH-nee): The classical music of North India.

jati (jetty): Patterns of hand and foot movements in bharata nāṭyam.

kaṇakku (kah-na-kuh): "Calculation." Rhythmic figures that create tension within the tāḷa they are designed to fit.

Karnatak (kar-NAH-tuck): The classical music of South India.

khaṇḍa cāpu tāḷa (con-da CHA-poo TAH-la): A five-beat tāḷa counted with claps on the first, third, and fourth beats.

konakkol (koe-nock-coal): Solkaṭṭu performed in a concert setting.

koraippu (ko-rye-pooh): "Reduction." A section of the tani āvartanam in which drummers trade progressively shorter groups of phrases.

kōrvai (CORE-way): A complex rhythmic design, ending with a mōrā.

laghu (la-goo): A tāḷa component, comprising a clap and finger counts.

meter: A regular arrangement of musical time.

miśra cāpu tāḷa (mish-ra CHA-poo TAH-la): A seven-beat tāḷa counted with claps on the first, fourth, and sixth beats.

mōrā (moe-rah): A rhythmic ending figure.

mrdangam (mri-dun-gum): The barrel-shaped, two-headed drum used to accompany Karnatak music.

naṭṭuvanar (not-two-vun-ahr): The dance master in a bharata nāṭyam ensemble.

Nāṭyaśāstra (NOT-ya-SHOSS-tra): The earliest known writing on Indian music, attributed to Bharata, 200 BCE–200 CE.

pallavi (pa-la-vee): In this text, a brief, rhythmically challenging song form designed for virtuosic improvisation. NB: The same word is used for the first section of the *kriti*, Karnatak music's main song form.

rūpaka tāḷa (ROO-pa-ka TAH-la): A three-beat tāḷa counted *clap clap wave*.

sarvalaghu (sar-va-la-goo): In general, rhythm patterns that carry the flow of musical time.

solkaṭṭu (soul-cut-two): The South Indian system of spoken syllables along with the hand gestures of a tāḷa.

suladi sapta tāḷa (soo-la-dee sup-ta TAH-la): A group of seven basic tāḷa structures, each of which can have five possible durations.

svara kalpana (sva-ra kal-pa-na): A form of melodic improvisation using solfege syllables.

tabla (tub-la): The pair of drums used to accompany Hindustani music.

tāḷa (TAH-la): A meter in Karnatak music, counted by recurring sets of hand gestures.

tani āvartanam (ta-nee AH-var-ta-num): The percussion solo in a Karnatak music concert.

tavil (tah-vill): An important percussion instrument in Karnatak music.

tīrmanam (TIER-ma-nam): A set composition in bharata nāṭyam, accompanied by solkaṭṭu.

tiśra jāti (tish-ra JAH-tee): The family of three-beat rhythms. Also, when referring to the *laghu*, three beats.

trikāla (tree-KAH-la): "Three speeds." A fundamental rhythmic process in Karnatak music.

tripuṭa tāḷa (tri-poo-tah TAH-la): One of the suladi sapta tāḷas. Its structure is one laghu and two *drutams* (clap and wave).

TIŚRA JĀTI ĒKA TĀḶA

1 · LESSONS, FIRST SERIES

Solkaṭṭu works by combining spoken rhythmic syllables into phrases and synchronizing these phrases with a stable tāḷa. Once the phrases and tāḷa are synchronized, a large repertoire of processes can be applied to the phrases: they may be sped up or slowed down, or expanded, contracted, or otherwise altered. The internal pulse grouping of beats in the tāḷa may also temporarily change to accommodate these processes. This series of lessons introduces some basic phrases and a simple tāḷa, along with exercises that demonstrate some of the fundamental processes.

Here are some basic phrases, from one to nine syllables in length; many others are possible. Where more than one example has been listed, they are separated by commas. **(01-001)**

one syllable: *ta, di, tom, nam, jem, tām*
two syllables: *ta ka, di mi, jo ṇu*
three syllables: *ta ki ṭa*
four syllables: *ta ka di mi, ta ka jo ṇu, ta ka di ku*
five syllables: *ta ka ta ki ṭa, ta di ki ṭa tom, ta din gi ṇa tom*
six syllables: *ta ka di mi ta ka, ta ki ṭa ta ki ṭa*
seven syllables: *ta ka di mi ta ki ṭa, ta ka ta di ki ṭa tom, ta ka ta din gi ṇa tom*
eight syllables: *ta ka di mi ta ka jo ṇu, ta ki ṭa ta di ki ṭa tom, ta ki ṭa ta din gi ṇa tom*
nine syllables: *ta ka di mi ta ka ta ki ṭa, ta ka di ku ta di ki ṭa tom, ta ka di ku ta din gi ṇa tom*

Longer phrases usually include rests. The use of rests will be introduced in the course of these lessons.

Tāḷas are made up of hand gestures, called *kriyā*. Nowadays only three kriyās are used: the clap (*taṭṭu*), which can be the palm of one hand against the other or against the thigh; the wave (*viccu*), which is often the back of the hand against the other or against the thigh; and finger counts, which always start from the pinky finger. Either the right or left hand may be used.

The introductory exercises that follow are set in *tiśra jāti ēka tāḷa,* a three-beat cycle made up of a clap and two finger counts as follows: clap, pinky finger, ring finger. This is the shortest cycle in the Karnatak system, which has roots reaching back more than two millennia. The Sanskrit word *tiśra* is a modernized version of the original *tryaśra*, meaning "three-sided." Thus a spatial metaphor underlies even modern notions of tāḷa.

All of the exercises and compositions in this book observe the same metric hierarchy: cycle, beat, and pulse. *Cycle* will indicate one full set of the hand gestures that manifest a particular tāḷa. *Beat* will refer to each of the gestures within the cycle, and *pulse* will describe the rate of the spoken syllables within each beat or cycle.

In the following exercises in tiśra jāti ēka tāḷa, each cycle comprises three beats. The process used in the first exercise will generate four pulses per beat.

The first exercises use the three-note phrase *ta ki ṭa*.

EXERCISE 1

With a metronome set at sixty, count through two cycles of tiśra jāti ēka tāḷa. Use only your hands: clap on beat one, move the pinky on beat two, and move the ring finger on beat three. Then speak the phrase along with the tāḷa, so that each syllable matches a hand gesture. Three syllables will take three beats or one full cycle. Do it four times, for four cycles. This is the first speed.

Next, keeping the metronome at sixty, double the speed of the spoken pattern while *keeping the speed of the tāḷa constant*. Now you are speaking two syllables in each beat, or six in each cycle. Do this also for four cycles. This is the second speed.

Finally, double the speed of the spoken phrases again. Now you have four syllables in each beat, and twelve in the cycle. Once again, do it for four cycles. This is the third speed.

The doubling and redoubling used in this exercise is called *trikāla,* literally "three speeds." Trikāla is perhaps the most fundamental of Karnatak music's rhythmic processes. It is found at every level of detail in every aspect of the music. In this case it serves three purposes: it reveals the four pulses per beat that characterize much Karnatak drumming; it introduces process-based tension within the tāḷa; and it suggests ways to notate this and the exercises that follow.

Four pulses per beat may be described as the *default* situation in Karnatak rhythm, but other pulse rates are possible and frequently used. Three, five, seven, and nine pulse-per-beat passages may appear even in a solo that starts and ends with four pulses per beat. The three-speed exercise starts out by matching each syllable to a beat. By doubling and redoubling the speed, it ends by matching the four pulses *within* each beat. The slowest speed, then, reveals the structure of the tala, while the fastest speed reveals the internal structure of the beat.

Because this doubling and redoubling is done within a three-beat cycle, the three-speed pattern introduces process-based tension within the tāḷa. When the speed of the original pattern is doubled, it is done twice within the three-beat cycle, requiring an accent at the beginning of the second pattern, at the *middle* of the cycle, where there is no hand gesture. When it is redoubled, the three-syllable pattern is performed four times within the three-beat cycle, requiring accents at each of the four *quarters* of the cycle, only the first of which coincides with a hand gesture. All of the exercises in this series exploit this tension, reinforcing accents at the middle and quarters of the cycle.

RHYTHMIC NOTATION IN KARNATAK MUSIC

Karnatak music is taught without the sort of prescriptive notation used in Euro-American traditions. The patterns and exercises can be written out, but there is no standard notation. Moreover, there is no consensus among Indian music scholars as to whether a beat is necessarily conceived of as articulated into pulses.

In the European tradition, which is often called *Western* music, rhythmic notation implies division into ever-smaller units. The whole note is equal to two half notes, four quarter notes, eight eighth notes, and so on. Karnatak music, by contrast, begins with the assumption that each beat is articulated into pulses. The first treatises on the subject define the duration of the fundamental beat (called *matra*) as "the time it takes to speak five short syllables." Not only does this definition indicate the oral nature of the tradition, it also introduces solkaṭṭu right from the beginning. Nowadays a given beat is assumed to comprise four pulses, but there are other possibilities.

How we express the three-speed exercise in notation depends on what we intend to do with it. For example, it could be shown with only the syllables, in which case we might represent the relative proportions of the speeds graphically. **(01-002N)**

We might simply indicate the process verbally, without a graphic aid: *ta ki ṭa* once per cycle, four times; *ta ki ṭa* twice per cycle, four times; *ta ki ṭa* four times per cycle, four times.

Perhaps the most useful notations make use of the four pulses per beat, revealed at the end of the process, in the notation at every speed. The utility of this approach will become clearer in later exercises. The following types of notation show the phrases and pulses, but not the tāḷa. They depend on a physical confidence of the performer in the relationship of tāḷa to phrase. In the first, each syllable is followed by three dashes, indicating a total value of four pulses. In the second, a subscript number takes the place of the dashes, indicating the pulse value of each syllable.

TYPE 1

ta - - - ki - - - ṭa - - - four times
ta - ki - ṭa - eight times
ta ki ṭa sixteen times

TYPE 2

ta_4 ki_4 $ṭa_4$ four times
ta_2 ki_2 $ṭa_2$ eight times
ta ki ṭa sixteen times

The most complete notation shows both tāḷa and pattern, and it uses the syllables and dashes shown as type 1 above. Such a complete notation is not necessary once the pattern and process are fully understood, but it will be useful in the early stages. **(01-003N)**

MIXED SPEED EXERCISES

Three exercises are made possible by mixing the second and third speeds from the three-speed exercise within a single cycle. One statement of the second speed (*ta - ki - ṭa -*) takes six pulses, as will two statements of the third speed (*ta ki ṭa ta ki ṭa*). As before, each of these should be performed in four-cycle groups.

EXERCISE 2

The first mixed-speed exercise begins with the second speed:
ta_2 ki_2 $ṭa_2$ ta ki ṭa ta ki ṭa, twelve pulses, one cycle **(01-004N)**

EXERCISE 3

The second mixed-speed exercise begins with the third speed:
ta ki ṭa ta ki ṭa ta_2 ki_2 $ṭa_2$, also twelve pulses and one cycle **(01-005N)**

EXERCISE 4

the third sandwiches the second speed between the two third-speed phrases:
ta ki ṭa ta_2 ki_2 $ṭa_2$ ta ki ṭa **(01-006N)**

Exercise 4 is the most challenging of the three. By placing the second-speed phrase in the middle, we have set this exercise up so that none of its syllables coincides with a beat. Remember that each beat is four pulses long, while each third-speed phrase has three pulses. This means that each third-speed phrase takes up three-quarters of a beat, so that the second-speed phrase begins on the last quarter of beat one. In terms of the notation, it means that beats two and three will fall on the "dashes," the unsounded pulses within the second speed pattern.

Practice Tip: If this exercise is challenging, try voicing the unsounded pulses as if they were extensions of the syllables' vowels, like this: ta *a* ki *i* ṭa *a*.

Two more mixed-speed exercises become possible if we invent a fourth version of our three-note phrase, one in which each syllable takes three pulses: ta_3 ki_3 $ṭa_3$. This phrase, while not generated by the three-speed exercise, is *suggested* by its sheer possibility. Much of the rhythmic innovation for which Karnatak musicians are so well known comes from uncovering patterns and treatments that are suggested by circumstances of meter and material.

The three-pulse-per-syllable version of our phrase is nine pulses long. Within a single cycle of twelve pulses, therefore, it can only be combined with a single third-speed phrase in one of two ways.

EXERCISE 5

ta_3 ki_3 $ṭa_3$ ta ki ṭa. **(01-007N)**

EXERCISE 6

ta ki ṭa ta_3 ki_3 $ṭa_3$. **(01-008N)**

The six exercises shown above exhaust the possibilities for a three-note phrase in a single three-beat cycle. They should all be practiced thoroughly as given. The next stage of this section repeats the same series of exercises, introducing the notion of a "rest" within the pattern. If one syllable is removed and replaced by a rest, the pattern is still three pulses long, but it only contains two sounded syllables. There are three possible phrases, shown here using the two-note phrase *ta ka* and a rest (•):

ta ka • **(01-009)**
ta • ka **(01-010)**
• ta ka **(01-011)**

The video examples show the trikāla only. Work out the other exercises for yourself, substituting these phrases.

Practice Tip: At the beginning, the rest should be voiced as an "m" sound in the chest. With practice this will naturally become faint, or perhaps fade away entirely, but it is important to use it in the early stages.

We have generated four versions of the three-note phrase *ta ki ṭa*, in which each syllable comprises four pulses, three pulses, two pulses, and one pulse. Each of the patterns and exercises to this point has been contained within a single cycle. The following design is generated by asking what happens if we make a pattern that uses all four versions of the phrase *but only once each*. The four-pulse version, which corresponds to our original first speed, takes twelve pulses; the three-pulse version takes nine; the two-pulse version takes six; and the fastest version takes three.

EXERCISE 7
ta - - - ki - - - ṭa - - - twelve
ta - - ki - - ṭa - - nine
ta - ki - ṭa - six
ta ki ṭa three **(01-012N)**

The resulting thirty-pulse figure does not fit evenly within the twelve-pulse cycle, so what purpose does it serve? It functions as a rhythmic design; this particular type, progressing from long to short, is called *gopucca*, or "cow's tail," and is perhaps the most widely used design type in Karnatak rhythm. It is an element of *kaṇakku*, or calculation, an important feature of Karnatak music whose significance will be developed throughout this book.

For now it is enough to take the term *calculation* literally. For example, let us say that we want this figure to *end* coincidentally with the tāḷa. Because it takes thirty pulses, it cannot *begin* with the tāḷa; its pulse total would have to be an even multiple of twelve. The nearest multiple of twelve to thirty is thirty-six, three cycles of the tāḷa. It begins after six pulses, or halfway through a cycle. Try it, waiting six pulses to begin. At the end of the pattern, when the tāḷa recycles to beat one, say *tām* on that first beat.

A natural question arises: how does one know when to start?

Practice Tip: Don't count in numbers, count in *syllables*. There are two ways to count six pulses using syllables: once through the second speed, *ta - ki - ṭa -;* or twice through the third speed, *ta ki ṭa ta ki ṭa*. Counting in syllables, besides being good practice, will be good preparation for later stages, in which unvoiced material can easily be transformed into voiced material. **(01-012N) (01-013)**

Why that *tām*? For the moment, think of it as the period at the end of a sentence, a signal that a design is complete. Its meaning will develop as the book progresses.

Having practiced this design thoroughly, try it with the other three three-note patterns:

ta ka • **(01-014)**
ta • ka **(01-015)**
• ta ka **(01-016)**

GLOSSARY

gopucca (go-put-cha): "Cow's tail." Rhythmic patterns that start long and get shorter.

kaṇakku (kah-na-kuh): "Calculation." Rhythmic figures that create tension within the tāḷa they are designed to fit.

kriyā (kree-YAH): The hand gestures used to count tāḷas.

taṭṭu (tut-two): The clap of one hand against the other or against the leg.

tiśra jāti ēka tāḷa (tish-ra JAH-tea ACHE-a TAH-la): The shortest tāḷa in the Karnatak system, a three-beat cycle made up of a clap and two finger counts.

tryaśra (tree-ash-ra): "Three sides." The class of tāḷas based on three.

viccu (vee-choo): The wave of one hand away from the other or from the leg.

2 · LESSONS, SECOND SERIES

This series of lessons combines some of the phrases from the first series into longer phrases and arranges these into a rudimentary rhythmic *composition* that follows the course of a typical Karnatak drumming idea. Begin by using the first two variations of the original three-note phrase, *ta ka* • and *ta* • *ka*. In this and following sections, the asterisk (*) is used as a multiplication sign.

Second Series, Pattern 1 **(02-017N)**

Let ta • ka = a, ta ka • = b. Combine these into two phrases, *ab* (ta • ka ta ka •) and *ba* (ta ka • ta • ka).

STAGE I

{7*ab + 1*ba} * 2, eight cycles total

Notice that each of the phrase groups is six pulses long, so that two of them will fit into one cycle of the tāḷa. This stage comprises eight of the groups, or four cycles. Do it twice. By reversing the order of the phrases at the end of the fourth cycle, we give a simple shape to the four-cycle group. By repeating the section, we are making this shape clearly identifiable. **(02-017)**

STAGE II

{3*ab + 1*ba} * 2, four cycles total

This stage brings in the reversed phrase twice as frequently, suggesting that it is gaining importance. Again, repeating the section reinforces the significance of the reversed phrase. **(02-018)**

STAGE III

{ab + ba} * 4, four cycles total

Now the reversed phrase ends each cycle, and momentum continues to build. **(02-019)**

STAGE IV

{ba} * 4, two cycles total

At this point the *ab* phrase has disappeared in favor of the ending phrase, *ba*. This is the first stage to occupy fewer than four cycles. **(02-020)**

STAGE V.

{b} ∗ 4 + *tām,* one cycle **(02-021)**

The relatively complex arrangement of phrases in stage I is here reduced to the third speed of the first exercise in the previous series. The final *tām,* as in exercise 7 in the previous series, serves as a signal that the pattern has run its course. In this series that *tām* will be used differently. Before explaining the difference, let us change the phrases slightly, replacing the sound *ka* with the arguably more sonorous *din*, as will follow in pattern 2.

Second Series, Pattern 2 **(02-027N)**

Change the phrases: a = din • ta, b = ta din •. Now perform the entire pattern, nineteen cycles in all, using the new phrases.

STAGE I

{7∗ab + 1∗ba} ∗ 2 **(02-022)**

STAGE II

{3∗ab + 1∗ba} ∗ 2 **(02-023)**

STAGE III

{ab + ba} ∗ 4 **(02-024)**

STAGE IV

{ba} ∗ 4 **(02-025)**

STAGE V

{b} ∗ 4 + *tām* **(02-026)**

Up to the final *tām*, all the patterns so far fit the definition of *sarvalaghu*, patterns that reinforce and enhance the flow of musical time. Even though the six-note phrases above exhibit the same process-based tension that was set up in the first series of exercises, their main function is to organize and embellish the time-flow. Sarvalaghu patterns are used to set up designs, called *mōrās* and *kōrvais*, that exemplify the concept *kaṇakku*, or calculation. We have already seen an example of such a design in exercise 7 in the first series.

MŌRĀ: THE FUNDAMENTAL KAṆAKKU DESIGN

Mōrā describes a way of organizing rhythmic phrases so that they function as endings: of cycles, of musical passages, and of rhythmic compositions. In mrdangam accompaniment, a mōrā is used to mark sections of songs or to draw the listener's attention to structural points in the tāḷa or song text. In *svara kalpana* improvisation a singer or instrumentalist may use a mōrā, set to a melody, as the finale of a passage. In percussion solo playing, mōrās are used in motivic development and to end kōrvais, more elaborate ending compositions that will be discussed in a later section.

The mōrā's form is deceptively simple, with implications that, as we will see in later chapters, might be described as *fractal*. By this I mean that the same structure can be found at increasingly complex levels of scale. In its essential form the mōrā is made up of a phrase, stated three times, with separations, called gaps, inserted among the statements as follows: (statement) [gap] (statement) [gap] (statement). We will abbreviate these as (s) and [g], with the following properties:

(s) ≥ 1 (syllable) The *statement* must state something consisting of at least one syllable

[g] ≥ 0 (pulse) The *gap* may be zero or greater, and, if greater than zero, may be sounded or unsounded

The notion of the gap requires some explanation. Let us take as an example a mōrā with the following structure: (s) = *ta di ki ṭa tom,* [g] = 0, for a total duration of fifteen pulses, as follows:

(ta di ki ṭa tom) [0] (ta di ki ṭa tom) [0] (ta di ki ṭa tom)

We will perform it in *caturaśra jāti ēka tāḷa*, the four-beat version of the three-beat tāḷa we have used so far. If we assume four pulses in each beat, this fifteen-pulse mōrā will occupy all but one of the pulses of the cycle. Remember that the mōrā is an *ending* figure. So we will leave one silent pulse at the beginning of the cycle and use the mōrā to finish the remaining fifteen pulses. The double lines in the next two examples represent the beginnings of cycles, while the single lines represent beats within each cycle.

II • (ta di ki I ṭa tom) [0] (ta di I ki ṭa tom) [0] (ta I di ki ṭa tom) II **(03-028)**

We can take the same statement and increase the gap from zero to one silent pulse. Because the gap happens twice (and both occurrences must be the same duration), this will add two pulses to the mōrā's duration, for a total of seventeen, as shown below. The seventeen-pulse duration is now too long for a single cycle, so the example shows *two* cycles, with the first fifteen pulses of the first cycle indicated by dots:

II • • • • I • • • • I • • • • I • • • (ta II di ki ṭa tom) I [•] (ta di ki I ṭa tom) [•] (taI di ki ṭa tom) II **(03-029)**

Since the mōrā is one pulse longer than our sixteen-pulse cycle, it begins one pulse *before* the first beat. This process of expansion can go on indefinitely, within limits of time and aesthetic suitability.

It is a practical fact of Karnatak rhythmic behavior that if a mōrā statement is shorter than five pulses, its gap will nearly always be at least two pulses and will include some articulations. The most extreme example of this feature is a statement that is one pulse in length. We can express this as s = 1, *(ta)*; g = 2, *[tām •]*. The resulting mōrā, a total of seven pulses, looks like this:

(ta) [tām •] (ta) [tām •] (ta)

This is the simplest possible mōrā where (s) = 1. It is not included merely for theoretical reasons; we will use it to complete the composition that began this section.

Such a small mōrā is mainly used in motivic development. Beginning with this seven-pulse mōrā, we will generate a *series* of simple mōrās to complete our composition. We will do so by increasing the statement by one pulse each time, while leaving the gap at two, *[tām •]*.

Remember that each cycle of tiśra ēka tāḷa has twelve pulses. Since our small mōrā is seven pulses long and must end the cycle, we must add another cycle after stage V. Adding a four-pulse rest will extend the syllable *tām*, which we were using to end stage V. This will be followed by the seven-pulse mōrā.

STAGE V

{b}*4 + tām • • • • + mōrā 1, (ta) [tām •] (ta) [tām •] (ta) **(03-030)**

Remember to count in syllables, not in numbers. Silent syllables can be voiced at any time to change the aesthetic effect. But what silent syllables should we use?

Because *tām* is a long syllable, almost always at least two pulses, we can start with *tām* •. We need to add three syllables to make up our five-pulse figure. Use the original three-note phrase *ta ki ṭa*.

Our five-pulse figure can be conceived as *tām • ta ki ṭa*. Voice the whole phrase to begin with, letting the *ta ki ṭa* get softer until it becomes silent. Do not rush this process; let it happen naturally.

Mōrā Series 1, Mōrā 1

Now speak the entire composition from the beginning, ending with mōrā 1. **(03-031N)**

GLOSSARY

caturaśra jāti ēka tāḷa (cha-TOOSH-ra JAH-tea ACHE-a TAH-la): A four-beat cycle made up of a clap followed by three finger counts.

kōrvai (CORE-way): A complex rhythmic design ending with a mōrā.

mōrā (moe-rah): A rhythmic ending figure made with the form (statement) [gap] (statement) [gap] (statement).

sarvalaghu (sar-va-la-goo): In general, rhythm patterns that carry the flow of musical time.

3 · MŌRĀ SERIES 1

Here is the composition so far, including the first mōrā. In the interest of space, the notation in the text from this point on will use subscript numbers instead of dots to indicate rests. Thus *$tām_5$* will take the place of *tām* • • • • and *[$tām_2$]* will take the place of *[tām •]*. The accompanying tāḷa notations will continue to use dashes.

Mōrā Series 1, Mōrā 1 **(03-031N)**

STAGE I

{7*ab + 1*ba} * 2

STAGE II

{3*ab + 1*ba} * 2

STAGE III

{ab + ba} * 4

STAGE IV

{ba} * 4

STAGE V

{b}*4 + $tām_5$ + mōrā 1, (ta) [$tām_2$] (ta) [$tām_2$] (ta) *tām*

Developing a motivic series requires aesthetic and practical choices. Throughout this book we will observe an important compositional principle: avoid changing too much at one time. If we keep our changes clear and consistent, the underlying idea comes more easily to the foreground.

In this case we will proceed by expanding the statement by one pulse in each new mōrā, leaving the gap unchanged. In mōrā 2, the statement increases to two pulses, *din ta*: s = 2, (din ta). The new mōrā, then, is (din ta) [$tām_2$] (din ta) [$tām_2$] (din ta), ten pulses total.

Because there are three statements, and we are increasing each by one pulse, the new mōrā is longer than the first one by three pulses, as (s) now equals two. It has to start three pulses earlier, since the mōrā functions as an *ending*, with its last syllable as the last syllable in the cycle. We must therefore shorten the preceding material by three pulses.

In order to find the best way to do this, we must keep two things in mind. First, this is a motivic development—we want a *series* of mōrās, so this process will be repeated. We are going to *add* three pulses within each mōrā and therefore must find a way to *remove* three pulses each time from the material preceding the mōrā. Second, it will be helpful if we can find a way to apply the same process in order to arrive at the starting point for each of the mōrās in the series.

Notice that the *b* figure stated four times in stage V is three pulses long. If we simply drop one of these figures, the five-pulse *tām* and the mōrā are shifted back by the necessary three pulses.

STAGE V

{b}∗3 + tām_5 + mōrā 2, (din ta) [tām_2] (din ta) [tām_2] (din ta) **(03-032)**

Since these mōrās will be performed as a series, there is no need to repeat the entire setup for mōrā 2. Repeat the setup from stage III, as follows:

STAGE I

{7∗ab + 1∗ba} ∗ 2

STAGE II

{3∗ab + 1∗ba} ∗ 2

STAGE III

{ab + ba} ∗ 4

STAGE IV

{ba} ∗ 4

STAGE V

{b}∗4 + tām_5 + mōrā 1, (ta) [tām_2] (ta) [tām_2] (ta), repeat to stage III

Mōrā Series 1, Mōrā 2 **(03-033N)**

STAGE III

{ab + ba} ∗ 4

STAGE IV

{ba} ∗ 4

STAGE V

{b}∗3 + tām_5 + mōrā 2, (din ta) [tām_2] (din ta) [tām_2] (din ta)

The third mōrā follows the same logic. The statement increases by one pulse, so $s = 3$ (ka din ta), and the mōrā is now thirteen pulses. Note that this is one pulse longer than the twelve-pulse cycle, so the mōrā begins on the last pulse of the preceding cycle. Once again, one *{b}* must be omitted from stage V, as follows:

STAGE V

{b}∗2 + tām_5 + mōrā 3, (ka din ta) [tām_2] (ka din ta) [tām_2] (ka din ta)

And as before, repeat the setup only from stage III, as follows:

STAGE I

{7*ab + 1*ba} * 2

STAGE II

{3*ab + 1*ba} * 2

STAGE III

{ab + ba} * 4

STAGE IV

{ba} * 4

STAGE V

{b}*4 + $tām_5$ + mōrā 1, (ta) [$tām_2$] (ta) [$tām_2$] (ta), repeat to stage III

STAGE III

{ab + ba} * 4

STAGE IV

{ba} * 4

STAGE V

{b}*3 + $tām_5$ + mōrā 2, (din ta) [$tām_2$] (din ta) [$tām_2$] (din ta), repeat to stage III

Mōrā Series 1, Mōrā 3 **(03-034N)**

STAGE III

{ab + ba} * 4

STAGE IV

{ba} * 4

STAGE V

{b}*2 + $tām_5$ + mōrā 3, (ka din ta) [$tām_2$] (ka din ta) [$tām_2$] (ka din ta)

The fourth mōrā follows logically: s = 4 *(ta ka din ta),* so the total is sixteen pulses. Now stage V only keeps one *{b},* as follows:

STAGE V

{b} + $tām_5$ + mōrā 4, (ta ka din ta) [$tām_2$] (ta ka din ta) [$tām_2$] (ta ka din ta)

Here are all four mōrās, in series:

STAGE I

{7*ab + 1*ba} * 2

STAGE II

{3*ab + 1*ba} * 2

STAGE III

{ab + ba} * 4

STAGE IV

{ba} * 4

STAGE V

{b}*4 + tām_5 + mōrā 1, (ta) [tām_2] (ta) [tām_2] (ta), repeat to stage III

STAGE III

{ab + ba} * 4

STAGE IV

{ba} * 4

STAGE V

{b}*3 + tām_5 + mōrā 2, (din ta) [tām_2] (din ta) [tām_2] (din ta), repeat to stage III

STAGE III

{ab + ba} * 4

STAGE IV

{ba} * 4

STAGE V

{b}*2 + tām_5 + mōrā 3, (ka din ta) [tām_2] (ka din ta) [tām_2] (ka din ta), repeat to stage III

Mōrā Series 1, Mōrā 4 **(03-035N)**

STAGE III

{ab + ba} * 4

STAGE IV

{ba} * 4

STAGE V

{b} + tām_5 + mōrā 4, (ta ka din ta) [tām_2] (ta ka din ta) [tām_2] (ta ka din ta)

Exceptions to the Rule

Most mōrās can be expressed by the (s) [g] (s) [g] (s) paradigm. But, since this is music and not mathematics, exceptions are possible in some situations, as when an expansion or contraction is orderly and exhaustive. For example:

(ta ka din ta) [tām_2] (ka din ta) [tām_2] (din ta) [tām_2] (ta)

This example deviates from the paradigm in two important respects. First, it comprises four statements and three gaps. Second, the statements are not the same length. Even with these deviations, this is still considered a legitimate mōrā because it is orderly and exhaustive, as is its reverse:

(ta) [tām_2] (din ta) [tām_2] (ka din ta) [tām_2] (ta ka din ta)

Each of these is sixteen pulses, as is mōrā 4, and each uses the statements from all four mōrās. They will complete this motivic series.

STAGE I

{7*ab + 1*ba} * 2

STAGE II

{3*ab + 1*ba} * 2

STAGE III

{ab + ba} * 4

STAGE IV

{ba} * 4

STAGE V

{b}*4 + tām_5 + mōrā 1, (ta) [tām_2] (ta) [tām_2] (ta), repeat to stage III

STAGE III

{ab + ba} * 4

STAGE IV

{ba} * 4

STAGE V

{b}*3 + tām_5 + mōrā 2, (din ta) [tām_2] (din ta) [tām_2] (din ta), repeat to stage III

STAGE III

{ab + ba} * 4

STAGE IV

{ba} * 4

STAGE V

{b}*2 + tām_5 + mōrā 3, (ka din ta) [tām_2] (ka din ta) [tām_2] (ka din ta), repeat to stage III

STAGE III

{ab + ba} * 4

STAGE IV

{ba} * 4

STAGE V

{b} + $tām_5$ + mōrā 4, (ta ka din ta) [$tām_2$] (ta ka din ta) [$tām_2$] (ta ka din ta), repeat to stage III

Mōrā Series 1, Mōrā 5 **(03-036N)**

STAGE III

{ab + ba} * 4

STAGE IV

{ba} * 4

STAGE V

{b} + $tām_5$ + mōrā 5, (ta ka din ta) [$tām_2$] (ka din ta) [$tām_2$] (din ta) [$tām_2$] (ta), repeat to stage III

Mōrā Series 1, Mōrā 6 **(03-037N)**

STAGE III

{ab + ba} * 4

STAGE IV

{ba} * 4

STAGE V

{b} + $tām_5$ + mōrā 6, (ta) [$tām_2$] (din ta) [$tām_2$] (ka din ta) [$tām_2$] (ta ka din ta) **tām**

These six mōrās complete the first series. When performed in sequence, they show an orderly development from one-syllable to four-syllable statements and provide examples of allowable exceptions to the mōrā paradigm. The next series will keep the statement intact and expand the gaps.

4 · MŌRĀ SERIES 2

The second series of mōrās is built on the same basic structure as the first series, at least through stage IV:

STAGE I
{7*ab + 1*ba} * 2

STAGE II
{3*ab + 1*ba} * 2

STAGE III
{ab + ba} * 4

STAGE IV
{ba} * 4

Again, this is a motivic series; the mōrās are designed to be performed in succession.

This series proceeds by expanding the gaps in the successive mōrās, leaving the statement at the one-pulse *(ta)*. The gaps increase from two pulses, *[tām$_2$]*, to four, *[tām$_4$]*, to six, *[tām$_6$]*, to eight, *[tām$_8$]*, and finally to ten *[tām$_{10}$]*. This means that each successive mōrā's duration will increase by four pulses.

The treatment of stage V must change to suit the new expansion. In the previous series we took advantage of the fact that each of the four *b* figures in stage V was three pulses long. In this series we will make use of the fact that there are *four* groups in stage V and remove one pulse at a time from each to arrive at the correct starting point.

To heighten the focus on "fourness," articulate only the first syllable of each group and use the four-syllable phrase *ta ka di mi* for these articulations, as follows:

ta din - **ta** din - **ta** din - **ta** din - becomes ta$_3$ ka$_3$ di$_3$ mi$_3$

Remember that the extra pulses after a syllable actually belong to and lengthen that syllable. It may be helpful to pronounce the new twelve-pulse figure as follows:

ta *a a* **ka** *a a* **di** *i i* **mi** *i i* **(04-038)**

Because the new series emphasizes the increasing silence, or space, of the gaps, we will articulate the five-pulse tām that preceded each of the first-series mōrās in order to heighten the contrast, as follows:

tām$_5$ becomes ta ka ta ki ṭa

When we incorporate these changes into stage V, the setup for the first mōrā in the second series is ta$_3$ ka$_3$ di$_3$ mi$_3$ ta ka ta ki ṭa. The first mōrā is the same as in series 1, s = 1, *(ta)*, g = 2, *[tām$_2$]*, and therefore starts in the same place, on the second pulse of beat two in the last cycle.

The new stage V + mōrā 1:
ta$_3$ ka$_3$ di$_3$ mi$_3$ ta ka ta ki ṭa + (ta) [tām$_2$] (ta) [tām$_2$] (ta)

Here is the composition so far, including the first mōrā in series 2:

Mōrā Series 2, Mōrā 1 **(04-039N)**

STAGE I
{7∗ab + 1∗ba} ∗ 2

STAGE II
{3∗ab + 1∗ba} ∗ 2

STAGE III
{ab + ba} ∗ 4

STAGE IV
{ba} ∗ 4

STAGE V + MŌRĀ 1
ta$_3$ ka$_3$ di$_3$ mi$_3$ ta ka ta ki ṭa + (ta) [tām$_2$] (ta) [tām$_2$] (ta)

The second mōrā leaves the statement alone, s = 1 *(ta)*, while the gap increases to *[tām$_4$]*.

Practice Tip: It is easiest to count the long gaps in this series of mōrās at half speed. For example, the four-pulse *tām$_4$* may be voiced as *tām - m -*.

Since each gap increases by two pulses for a total of four pulses, we remove one pulse each from *ta$_3$ ka$_3$ di$_3$ mi$_3$*. Stage V for the second mōrā thus becomes *ta$_2$ ka$_2$ di$_2$ mi$_2$ ta ka ta ki ṭa.*

Stage V + mōrā 2 is now ta$_2$ ka$_2$ di$_2$ mi$_2$ ta ka ta ki ṭa + (ta) [tām$_4$] (ta) [tām$_4$] (ta). Since the mōrā is longer than mōrā 1 by four pulses, it starts exactly one beat earlier, on the second pulse of beat one in the last cycle.

As was the case with mōrā series 1, repeat back to stage III in performing this series.

STAGE I
{7∗ab + 1∗ba} ∗ 2

STAGE II

{3∗ab + 1∗ba} ∗ 2

STAGE III

{ab + ba} ∗ 4

STAGE IV

{ba} ∗ 4

STAGE V + MŌRĀ 1

ta_3 ka_3 di_3 mi_3 + ta ka ta ki ṭa + (ta) [$tām_2$] (ta) [$tām_2$] (ta), back to stage III

Mōrā Series 2, Mōrā 2 **(04-040N)**

STAGE III

{ab + ba} ∗ 4

STAGE IV

{ba} ∗ 4

STAGE V + MŌRĀ 2

ta_2 ka_2 di_2 mi_2 + ta ka ta ki ṭa + (ta) [$tām_4$] (ta) [$tām_4$] (ta), back to stage III

The third mōrā increases the gap to [$tām_6$]. Voice this gap as if it were a slow three, *tām - m - m -*. Stage V for mōrā 3 removes all the rests from *ta ka di mi*: now the pattern leading into the mōrā is *ta ka di mi ta ka ta ki ṭa*.

Stage V + mōrā 3 is ta ka di mi + ta ka ta ki ṭa + (ta) [$tām_6$] (ta) [$tām_6$] (ta). As was the case with mōrā 2, the four-pulse expansion of the gaps means that it starts one full beat earlier, on the second pulse of beat three in the next-to-last cycle.

Mōrā Series 2, Mōrā 3 **(04-041N)**

Here are the first three mōrās in sequence:

STAGE I

{7∗ab + 1∗ba} ∗ 2

STAGE II

{3∗ab + 1∗ba} ∗ 2

STAGE III

{ab + ba} ∗ 4

STAGE IV

{ba} ∗ 4

STAGE V + MŌRĀ 1

ta_3 ka_3 di_3 mi_3 + ta ka ta ki ṭa + (ta) [$tām_2$] (ta) [$tām_2$] (ta), back to stage III

STAGE III

{ab + ba} * 4

STAGE IV

{ba} * 4

STAGE V + MŌRĀ 2

ta_2 ka_2 di_2 mi_2 + ta ka ta ki ṭa + (ta) [$tām_4$] (ta) [$tām_4$] (ta), back to stage III

STAGE III

{ab + ba} * 4

STAGE IV

{ba} * 4

STAGE V + MŌRĀ 3

ta ka di mi + ta ka ta ki ṭa + (ta) [$tām_6$] (ta) [$tām_6$] (ta), back to stage III

The fourth mōrā increases the gap to [$tām_8$]. Voice this gap as if it were a slow four, *tām - m - m - m -*. Stage V now eliminates *ta ka di mi* completely, leaving only *ta ka ta ki ṭa.*

Stage V + mōrā 4 is *ta ka ta ki ṭa + (ta) [$tām_8$] (ta) [$tām_8$] (ta).* This mōrā starts on the second pulse of beat two in the next-to-last cycle.

Mōrā Series 2, Mōrā 4 **(04-042N)**

The first four mōrās:

STAGE I

{7*ab + 1*ba} * 2

STAGE II

{3*ab + 1*ba} * 2

STAGE III

{ab + ba} * 4

STAGE IV

{ba} * 4

STAGE V + MŌRĀ 1

ta_3 ka_3 di_3 mi_3 + ta ka ta ki ṭa + (ta) [$tām_2$] (ta) [$tām_2$] (ta), back to stage III

STAGE III

{ab + ba} * 4

STAGE IV

{ba} * 4

STAGE V + MŌRĀ 2

ta_2 ka_2 di_2 mi_2 + ta ka ta ki ṭa + (ta) [$tām_4$] (ta) [$tām_4$] (ta), back to stage III

STAGE III

{ab + ba} * 4

STAGE IV

{ba} * 4

STAGE V + MŌRĀ 3

ta ka di mi + ta ka ta ki ṭa + (ta) [$tām_6$] (ta) [$tām_6$] (ta), back to stage III

STAGE III

{ab + ba} * 4

STAGE IV

{ba} * 4

STAGE V + MŌRĀ 4

ta ka ta ki ṭa + (ta) [$tām_8$] (ta) [$tām_8$] (ta), back to stage III

The fifth and last mōrā increases the gap to [$tām_{10}$]. Voice this gap as if it were a slow five, *tām - m - m - m - m -*. Since all that remains of stage V is the five-pulse *ta ka ta ki ṭa*, remove four pulses and replace *ta* with a rest. This mōrā starts immediately after this rest, on the second pulse of the first beat in the next-to-last cycle.

Mōrā Series 2, Mōrā 5 **(04-043)**

stage V + mōrā 5: • (ta) [$tām_{10}$] (ta) [$tām_{10}$] (ta)

Here is the entire series of five mōrās:

STAGE I

{7*ab + 1*ba} * 2

STAGE II

{3*ab + 1*ba} * 2

STAGE III

{ab + ba} * 4

STAGE IV

{ba} * 4

STAGE V + MŌRĀ 1

ta_3 ka_3 di_3 mi_3 + ta ka ta ki ṭa + (ta) [$tām_2$] (ta) [$tām_2$] (ta), back to stage III

STAGE III

{ab + ba} * 4

STAGE IV
{ba} * 4

STAGE V + MŌRĀ 2
ta_2 ka_2 di_2 mi_2 + ta ka ta ki ṭa + (ta) [$tām_4$] (ta) [$tām_4$] (ta), back to stage III

STAGE III
{ab + ba} * 4

STAGE IV
{ba} * 4

STAGE V + MŌRĀ 3
ta ka di mi + ta ka ta ki ṭa + (ta) [$tām_6$] (ta) [$tām_6$] (ta), back to stage III

STAGE III
{ab + ba} * 4

STAGE IV
{ba} * 4

STAGE V + MŌRĀ 4
ta ka ta ki ṭa + (ta) [$tām_8$] (ta) [$tām_8$] (ta), back to stage III

STAGE III
{ab + ba} * 4

STAGE IV
{ba} * 4

STAGE V + MŌRĀ 5
• (ta) [$tām_{10}$] (ta) [$tām_{10}$] (ta) **tām**

These two series of simple mōrās have introduced the fundamental components of the mōrā, statement and gap, and have demonstrated their use as motivic figures within structures of *sarvalaghu*, or time-flow figures. Because each series progresses by expanding either the statement or the gap while leaving the other intact, they have also demonstrated the aesthetic device of changing one thing at a time for the sake of clarity. The next section will introduce much longer statements and more challenging mōrās designed to build rhythmic strength and confidence.

II EXERCISE MŌRĀS

5 · FOUR EXERCISE MŌRĀS

Exercise Mōrā 1: Tiśra Jāti Ēka Tāḷa

The exercise mōrās in this section are designed to develop rhythmic confidence in dealing with what we may call *offbeat* accents. The shapes of the phrases, combined with the mōrā form, result in accents that seem to fall in unexpected places. With practice, however, the placement of these accents will be revealed as quite logical, and the beauty generated by this logical metric tension will shine through. Through practicing these mōrās, the once-challenging quarters of cycles made up of odd numbers of beats such as three, five, seven, and nine will become manageable, if not quite comfortable.

All the exercise mōrās make use of statements in the *gopucca* shape. The first one uses the same thirty-pulse pattern as exercise 7 in the first lesson series:

(ta • • • ki • • • ṭa • • •
ta • • ki • • ṭa • •
ta • ki • ṭa •
ta ki ṭa)

In exercise 7 we conceived this figure as four versions of the phrase *ta ki ṭa*. Now the entire figure becomes the statement in a mōrā. Its thirty pulses are stated three times, for ninety total pulses. If we add six pulses, the total is ninety-six, exactly eight cycles of the twelve-pulse tiśra jāti ēka tāḷa. We can easily add these as two gaps of three pulses each, [tām • •]. So (s) = 30, [g] = 3. Here it is, notated within the tāḷa.

EXERCISE MŌRĀ 1 **(05-044N)**

Most people will find this mōrā challenging, especially its second statement. Though it may seem counterintuitive to do so, the most efficient way to learn this mōrā is to start from the end and work backward. What follows is a step-by-step exposition of this process. I strongly recommend that you work through the first mōrā using this method. It may not be necessary to be so rigorous with the others, but this method can always be used when you are stuck. It will be helpful to keep the notation handy while working backward through the mōrā. Be sure to recite all the way through to the end as you add each phrase. This will reinforce your command of the material at every stage.

The graphic notation for exercise mōrā 1 will help you to understand the step-by-step account below. Remember that every phrase in this mōrā's statements is some version of *ta ki ṭa*; therefore, every phrase will start on one of the "quarters" of the cycle. In the following explanation, silent phrases are italicized and bracketed, for example *{ta ki ṭa ta ki ṭa ta ki ṭa}*.

1. The very last phrase is *ta ki ṭa*. Count your way in by counting three sets of third-speed *ta ki ṭa* silently, then voicing the last one:

{ta ki ṭa ta ki ṭa ta ki ṭa} ta ki ṭa

2. Now add the next-to-last phrase, *ta • ki • ṭa • ta ki ṭa*. The two phrases together are nine pulses; start after one silent *ta ki ṭa,* on the last pulse of beat one:

{ta ki ṭa} ta • ki • ṭa • ta ki ṭa

Notice that this is very similar to exercise 4 in the first section, but with the first third-speed *ta ki ṭa* unvoiced.

3. Next, add the nine-pulse *ta • • ki • • ṭa • •*. Notice that the last three-pulse syllable *ṭa • •* falls on the first beat of the last cycle. It follows that the preceding six pulses, *ta • • ki • •*, will begin in the middle of the preceding cycle, after six silent syllables.

{ta ki ṭa ta ki ṭa} ta • • ki • • ṭa • • ta • ki • ṭa • ta ki ṭa

4. Since the twelve-pulse *ta • • • ki • • • ṭa • • •* that begins the last statement takes a full cycle, it begins at the same point as the nine-pulse phrase, again after six silent pulses.

{ta ki ṭa ta ki ṭa} ta • • • ki • • • ṭa • • • ta • • ki • • ṭa • • ta • ki • ṭa • ta ki ṭa

> *Practice Tip:* In all of the exercise mōrās, the second phrase of each statement will begin at the same point in the cycle as the first, because the first phrase is always one full cycle in duration.

5. Now add the second gap, *[tām • •]*. This begins on the second quarter of the cycle, after one third-speed *ta ki ṭa*.

{ta ki ṭa} [tām • •] ta • • • ki • • • ṭa • • • ta • • ki • • ṭa • • ta • ki • ṭa • ta ki ṭa

6. Coincidentally, this third-speed *ta ki ṭa* is the last phrase of the second statement.

ta ki ṭa [tām • •] ta • • • ki • • • ṭa • • • ta • • ki • • ṭa • • ta • ki • ṭa • ta ki ṭa

7. Adding the preceding six-pulse *ta • ki • ṭa •* is relatively easy, since it begins in the middle of the cycle. And the *ki • • ṭa • •* from the preceding nine-pulse phrase fills out the cycle.

8. This is where things get interesting. The *ta • •* that begins the nine-pulse phrase starts on the last quarter of the preceding cycle, on the second pulse of the third beat. As

we just pointed out, the preceding twelve-pulse *ta • • • ki • • • ṭa • • •* starts at the same point in the preceding cycle. This means that *all three syllables begin on the second pulse of their corresponding beats*. This is likely to be the most challenging stage, since the syllables come immediately after the hand gestures. Mastering this stage is the key to all of the exercise mōrās.

9. Now add the first gap, *[tām • •]*. This begins three pulses earlier, at the middle of the cycle.

10. Add the last phrase of the first statement, *ta ki ṭa*, which will begin on the second quarter of the cycle, again the last pulse of beat one.

11. The third phrase of statement one, the six-pulse *ta • ki • ṭa •*, starts on the second pulse of beat three in the preceding cycle.

12. The second phrase starts nine pulses earlier, on beat one.

13. And the first phrase, of course, begins on beat one and fills the first cycle.

I first encountered this exercise mōrā in the course of an interview with the legendary mrdangam master Palghat R. Raghu. We did not discuss it; he simply demonstrated it and said it could be used to "clear a lot of difficulties." I realized after some reflection that the structure of the mōrā he demonstrated could be used in other tāḷas, and that it could also be used with phrases using rests. These exercise mōrās have become really valuable in helping students to strengthen their control of offbeat accents and develop their sense of rhythmic form.

Work through the exercise mōrā using all four three-pulse phrases, *ta ki ṭa, ta ka •, ta • ka, • ta ka,* before going on to the exercise mōrās in other tāḷas. Tāḷa notation is provided for the first one only.

Exercise Mōrā 2: Khaṇḍa Jāti Ēka Tāḷa

The same logic that produced exercise mōrā 1 and its variations can generate similar mōrās for any tāḷa with an odd number of beats. There are two compositional rules: First, the number of syllables in the phrase must match the number of beats in the tāḷa. The statement will be analogous to the one we used in the first exercise mōrā, in that it will have four lines comprising four, three, two, and one pulse per syllable. Second, the gap must be one quarter of a cycle in duration. Put another way, the gap must be the same duration as a single third-speed version of the original phrase.

The tāḷa for exercise mōrā 2 is the five-beat cycle khaṇḍa jāti ēka tāḷa, counted by the following hand gestures: clap, pinky finger, ring finger, middle finger, index finger. The new phrase has five syllables, *ta ka ta ki ṭa*, and the gap has five pulses, *[tām$_5$]*.

The same seven exercises that we used to introduce tiśra ēka can be applied in order to acclimate yourself to the new tāḷa and syllables. Before attempting the new exercise mōrā, practice the following patterns in khaṇḍa jāti ēka tāḷa. Again in the interest of space, subscript numbers take the place of dots in this and the other exercise mōrā examples.

EXERCISE 1: THREE SPEEDS **(05-045)**

ta_4 ka_4 ta_4 ki_4 $ṭa_4$

ta_2 ka_2 ta_2 ki_2 $ṭa_2$ * 2

ta ka ta ki ṭa * 4

EXERCISE 2: SLOW FAST FAST **(05-046)**

ta_2 ka_2 ta_2 ki_2 $ṭa_2$ ta ka ta ki ṭa ta ka ta ki ṭa

EXERCISE 3: FAST FAST SLOW **(05-047)**

ta ka ta ki ṭa ta ka ta ki ṭa ta_2 ka_2 ta_2 ki_2 $ṭa_2$

EXERCISE 4: FAST SLOW FAST **(05-048)**

ta ka ta ki ṭa ta_2 ka_2 ta_2 ki_2 $ṭa_2$ ta ka ta ki ṭa

EXERCISE 5: THREE PLUS ONE **(05-049)**

ta_3 ka_3 ta_3 ki_3 $ṭa_3$ ta ka ta ki ṭa

EXERCISE 6: ONE PLUS THREE **(05-050)**

ta ka ta ki ṭa ta_3 ka_3 ta_3 ki_3 $ṭa_3$

EXERCISE 7: FOUR SPEEDS **(05-051)**

ta_4 ka_4 ta_4 ki_4 $ṭa_4$ ta_3 ka_3 ta_3 ki_3 $ṭa_3$ ta_2 ka_2 ta_2 ki_2 $ṭa_2$ ta ka ta ki ṭa

As was true of exercise 7 in the three-beat cycle, exercise 7 in the five-beat cycle takes two-and-a-half cycles and must start in the middle of the cycle.

QUARTERS OF THE CYCLE REVISITED

Remember that for exercise mōrā 1, the second and fourth quarters of the cycle fell just before beat two and just after beat three, because the three-note phrase was shorter than the four-pulse beat. In khaṇḍa jāti ēka tāḷa, the second and fourth quarters fall just after beat two and just before beat five, since the five-note phrase is longer than the beat by one pulse.

|| **ta** ka ta ki | ṭa **ta** ka ta | ki ṭa **ta** ka | ta ki ṭa **ta** | ka ta ki ṭa ||

EXERCISE MŌRĀ 2 **(05-052N)**

Look at the graphic notation. Count the five-pulse gap as if it were a phrase. Remember that in mōrā series 1, the five-pulse *tām* immediately preceding the mōrā was pronounced as if it were a phrase of two plus three, *tām • ta ki ṭa,* with the last three pulses whispered. Do the same in this case; at the beginning it may be helpful to articulate it without whispering. If necessary, work backward from the end, as you did with the first exercise mōrā.

Substitute the following five-note phrases for *ta ka ta ki ṭa* as skill allows, after first practicing them in the seven preparatory exercises:

din_2 ta ki ṭa

din_2 $tān_2$ gu

Notice that we are introducing only two variations for this mōrā. There are several other possibilities, any of which you might also try. These will suffice for the present, but feel free to experiment.

Exercise Mōrā 3: Miśra Jāti Ēka Tāḷa

The next exercise mōrā is in the seven-beat cycle miśra jāti ēka tāḷa, counted as follows: clap, pinky, ring, middle, index, thumb, pinky. Notice that the pinky finger is used twice, as beat two and again as beat seven.

The new phrase has seven syllables, *ta ka di mi ta ki ṭa,* and the gap has seven pulses, *[$tām_7$].* Count this gap with the phrase *tām • di mi ta ki ṭa.*

As you did with the previous tāḷas, practice seven corresponding preparatory exercises for miśra ēka tāḷa.

EXERCISE 1: THREE SPEEDS **(05-053)**
ta_4 ka_4 di_4 mi_4 ta_4 ki_4 $ṭa_4$
ta_2 ka_2 di_2 mi_2 ta_2 ki_2 $ṭa_2$ * 2
ta ka di mi ta ki ṭa * 4

EXERCISE 2: SLOW FAST FAST **(05-054)**
ta_2 ka_2 di_2 mi_2 ta_2 ki_2 $ṭa_2$ ta ka di mi ta ki ṭa ta ka di mi ta ki ṭa

EXERCISE 3: FAST FAST SLOW **(05-055)**
ta ka di mi ta ki ṭa ta ka di mi ta ki ṭa ta_2 ka_2 di_2 mi_2 ta_2 ki_2 $ṭa_2$

EXERCISE 4: FAST SLOW FAST **(05-056)**
ta ka di mi ta ki ṭa ta_2 ka_2 di_2 mi_2 ta_2 ki_2 $ṭa_2$ ta ka di mi ta ki ṭa

EXERCISE 5: THREE PLUS ONE **(05-057)**
ta_3 ka_3 di_3 mi_3 ta_3 ki_3 $ṭa_3$ ta ka di mi ta ki ṭa

EXERCISE 6: ONE PLUS THREE **(05-058)**
ta ka di mi ta ki ṭa ta_3 ka_3 di_3 mi_3 ta_3 ki_3 $ṭa_3$

EXERCISE 7: FOUR SPEEDS **(05-059)**
ta_4 ka_4 di_4 mi_4 ta_4 ki_4 $ṭa_4$
ta_3 ka_3 di_3 mi_3 ta_3 ki_3 $ṭa_3$
ta_2 ka_2 di_2 mi_2 ta_2 ki_2 $ṭa_2$
ta ka di mi ta ki ṭa

QUARTERS OF THE CYCLE
In this case the seven-pulse phrase falls one short of filling up two four-pulse beats. The second quarter falls on the last pulse of beat two (just before the ring finger), while the fourth quarter falls

on the second pulse of beat six (just after the thumb). The middle of the cycle falls between the middle and ring fingers.

|| **ta** ka di mi | ta ki ṭa **ta** | ka di mi ta | ki ṭa **ta** ka | di mi ta ki | ṭa **ta** ka di | mi ta ki ṭa ||

EXERCISE MŌRĀ 3 **(05-060N)**

Following the graphic notation, work through exercise mōrā 3, making use of the learning devices you used in the previous exercise mōrās. Substitute the following seven-note phrases for *ta ka di mi ta ki ṭa* as skill and time allow, after first practicing them in the seven preparatory exercises.

din$_2$ ta ka ta ki ṭa
din$_2$ ta$_2$ tān$_2$ gu

Exercise Mōrā 4: Saṅkīrṇa Jāti Ēka Tāḷa

The last group of exercise mōrās is set in saṅkīrṇa jāti ēka tāḷa, a nine-beat cycle counted as follows: clap, pinky, ring, middle, index, thumb, pinky, ring, middle.

Notice that the pinky, middle, and ring finger sequence happens twice in each cycle, as beats two, three, and four, and again as beats seven, eight, and nine. It takes alertness and concentration to avoid mixing them up.

The new phrase has nine syllables, *ta ka di mi ta ka ta ki ṭa,* and the gap has nine pulses, [*tām*$_9$]. This gap is significantly longer than the others. Count it either as **tām** • *di mi ta ka ta ki ṭa* or as **tām** • • *tām* • • *tām* • •.

The seven preparatory exercises for saṅkīrṇa ēka correspond to those for the other three tāḷas.

EXERCISE 1: THREE SPEEDS **(05-061)**

ta$_4$ ka$_4$ di$_4$ mi$_4$ ta$_4$ ka$_4$ ta$_4$ ki$_4$ ṭa$_4$
ta$_2$ ka$_2$ di$_2$ mi$_2$ ta$_2$ ka$_2$ ta$_2$ ki$_2$ ṭa$_2$ $*$ 2
ta ka di mi ta ka ta ki ṭa $*$ 4

EXERCISE 2: SLOW FAST FAST **(05-062)**

ta$_2$ ka$_2$ di$_2$ mi$_2$ ta$_2$ ka$_2$ ta$_2$ ki$_2$ ṭa$_2$ ta ka di mi ta ka ta ki ṭa ta ka di mi ta ka ta ki ṭa

EXERCISE 3: FAST FAST SLOW **(05-063)**

ta ka di mi ta ka ta ki ṭa ta ka di mi ta ka ta ki ṭa ta$_2$ ka$_2$ di$_2$ mi$_2$ ta$_2$ ka$_2$ ta$_2$ ki$_2$ ṭa$_2$

EXERCISE 4: FAST SLOW FAST **(05-064)**

ta ka di mi ta ka ta ki ṭa ta$_2$ ka$_2$ di$_2$ mi$_2$ ta$_2$ ka$_2$ ta$_2$ ki$_2$ ṭa$_2$ ta ka di mi ta ka ta ki ṭa

EXERCISE 5: THREE PLUS ONE **(05-065)**

ta$_3$ ka$_3$ di$_3$ mi$_3$ ta$_3$ ka$_3$ ta$_3$ ki$_3$ ṭa$_3$ ta ka di mi ta ka ta ki ṭa

EXERCISE 6: ONE PLUS THREE **(05-066)**

ta ka di mi ta ka ta ki ṭa ta$_3$ ka$_3$ di$_3$ mi$_3$ ta$_3$ ka$_3$ ta$_3$ ki$_3$ ṭa$_3$

EXERCISE 7: FOUR SPEEDS **(05-067)**

ta_4 ka_4 di_4 mi_4 ta_4 ka_4 ta_4 ki_4 $ṭa_4$
ta_3 ka_3 di_3 mi_3 ta_3 ka_3 ta_3 ki_3 $ṭa_3$
ta_2 ka_2 di_2 mi_2 ta_2 ka_2 ta_2 ki_2 $ṭa_2$
ta ka di mi ta ka ta ki ṭa

QUARTERS OF THE CYCLE

Since this is a nine-pulse phrase in a nine-beat cycle, the second quarter falls just after beat three (on its second pulse) and the fourth quarter just before beat eight (on the last pulse of beat seven). The middle of the cycle falls halfway through beat five, between the index finger and the thumb.

|| **ta** ka di mi | ta ka ta ki | ṭa **ta** ka di | mi ta ka ta | ki ṭa **ta** ka | di mi ta ka | ta ki ṭa **ta** |
ka di mi ta | ka ta ki ṭa ||

EXERCISE MŌRĀ 4 **(05-068N)**

Work through the mōrā following the graphic notation, using the learning tools you have acquired. Once the new exercise mōrā is well under control, substitute the following nine-note phrases for *ta ka di mi ta ka ta ki ṭa* as skill allows, after first practicing them in the seven preparatory exercises:

ta_2 din_2 ta ka ta ki ṭa
din_2 ta_2 $tān_2$ $tān_2$ gu

Including all of the variations, there are thirteen exercise mōrās in this section. These do not exhaust all of the possibilities, but they provide at least enough material for a one-semester course. Through conscientious practice, you will experience a distinct increase in your ability to control phrases and silence in challenging metric settings.

III ĀDI TĀḶA LESSONS

ĀDI TĀḶA AND THE STRUCTURE OF THE LESSONS

Ādi tāḷa is the most common tāḷa in South Indian music. At least 80 percent of Karnatak songs are set in this eight-beat meter. The name ādi *means "primordial," suggesting that it is much older than the thirty-five-tāḷa system, which probably dates back to the seventeenth century.*

According to the thirty-five-tāḷa system, the structure of ādi tāḷa is caturaśra jāti tripuṭa tāḷa, which means that its hand gestures comprise a laghu *of four counts and two* drutams *of two counts each:* **clap***, pinky, ring, middle,* **clap***, wave,* **clap***, wave. In South Indian drumming traditions, lessons beyond the rudimentary exercises always begin with this tāḷa. A student may continue in it for several years before moving to others. Whatever the tāḷa, lessons typically follow the form of the tani āvartanam, or Karnatak percussion solo.*

In its paradigm form, the structure of the tani can be understood as a series of designs (mōrās, kōrvais, etc.) set up by sarvalaghu figures that move from less densely articulated patterns at the beginning stages to increasingly dense and complex patterns as the solo progresses. During the course of the tani, mōrās, kōrvais, and even entire sections including sarvalaghu figures may be shifted into pulse groupings that differ from the original. The material that follows includes sections that shift from the original four-pulse-per-beat rate into three, six, and five pulses per beat.

Most of the material that follows could be performed by a single musician. Because this text is designed to be taught in a class or other group, however, there is also a koraippu*, a section meant to be shared by a group of musicians. And true to the tani paradigm, a stylized ending section concludes the piece.*

The tani āvartanam paradigm provides an elegant model for teaching the forms and processes of Karnatak rhythm. The material in the rest of this book should be viewed as constituting a single extended tani, in which each stage builds on the skills and understanding developed at the previous stage. More precisely, the material that follows could make up several tani āvartanams, each one constructed to fit a given performance situation. A section detailing some of these possible realizations follows the lessons; this section takes into account variables such as the number of performers, their skill levels, and the desired amount of time for the piece.

The following section provides many variations on each fundamental idea. How many of these are performed must be determined by the teacher and the ensemble. A typical Karnatak percussionist practices all of them, allowing the moment of performance to dictate which version to use.

GLOSSARY

caturaśra jāti tripuṭa tāḷa (cha-TOOSH-ra JAH-tea tri-poo-tah TAH-la): The name for ādi tāḷa as it occurs in the thirty-five-tāḷa scheme. It is made up of a four-beat *laghu* and two *drutams.*

drutam (dru-tam): A two-beat tāḷa component made up of a clap and a wave.

koraippu (ko-rye-pooh): "Reduction." A section of the tani āvartanam in which drummers trade progressively shorter groups of phrases.

laghu (la-goo): A tāḷa component comprising a clap and finger counts. The laghu may be three, four, five, seven, or nine beats long.

6 · ĀDI TĀḶA MŌRĀ SERIES 1

The opening section of our tani develops a mōrā series that includes variations, exceptions to rules that have been given so far, and examples of compound mōrās. This series of mōrās is based on *ta din din na*, the fundamental ādi tāḷa sarvalaghu pattern.

This four-syllable pattern is very similar in sound and effect to the tabla pattern used for *tīntāl*, Hindustani music's most common meter. But there are important differences between Hindustani and Karnatak time-flow patterns. In Hindustani music, the time-flow pattern *defines* the tāl, or meter, while the hand gestures are of secondary importance. In a very real sense, the Hindustani syllable pattern *is* the tāl.

In Karnatak music, by contrast, the *hand gestures* define the tāḷa, leaving the drummer free to use any number of patterns to embellish the movement of the music in time. We will use *ta din din na* as the opening sarvalaghu in this tani and develop other time-flow patterns in the sections that follow.

For this series we are assuming four pulses per beat in ādi tāḷa, or thirty-two pulses per cycle. Each syllable of the pattern is two pulses long, as follows:

ta_2 din_2 din_2 na_2

One thirty-two-pulse cycle requires four sets, the original and three variations:

a. ta_2 din_2 din_2 na_2
b. ta ka din_2 din_2 na_2
c. • • din_2 din_2 na_2
d. kṭtk din_2 din_2 na_2

Notice that line *d* introduces a new phrase, kṭtk

> *Notation Convention:* Vowels are removed for double time. The figure *kṭtk* is short for *ki ṭa ta ka*; the omission of the vowels indicates that it is to be pronounced at twice the speed of the fully spelled-out pattern. So the four-note figure *kṭtk,* without vowels, is pronounced in the time of two regular syllables.

The phrase that will become the mōrā statement is introduced as pattern *e*: note that it also contains a double time figure, *kṭ,* that stands for *ki ṭa.*

e. • • ta ta kṭ tom tom ta

Using the same principle we employed in tiśra jāti ēka mōrā series 1 and 2, we will set up the time-flow figures *a, b, c,* and *d* to introduce figure *e* at the end of a two-cycle group. We will call this stage I.

STAGE I **(06-069)**
a. ta_2 din_2 din_2 na_2
b. ta ka din_2 din_2 na_2
c. • • din_2 din_2 na_2
d. kṭtk din_2 din_2 na_2

a. ta_2 din_2 din_2 na_2
b. ta ka din_2 din_2 na_2
c. • • din_2 din_2 na_2
e. • • ta ta kṭ tom tom ta

Do this group, {abcd abce}, twice.

STAGE II **(06-070)**
Stage II comprises just the second half of stage I, {abce}, introducing *ta ta kṭ tom tom ta* at the end of each cycle. Do this stage twice.

STAGE III **(06-071)**
Stage III introduces the phrase at the end of each half cycle, using each of the sarvalaghu variations once, {aebecede}.

Here is the composition so far:

STAGE I
{abcd abce}, twice

STAGE II
{abce}, twice

STAGE III
{aebecede}

Now we can add the first mōrā. Its statement is the six-pulse *ta ta kṭ tom tom ta* but without the two-pulse rest that made it fit so neatly into the sarvalaghu setup.

s = 6, (ta ta kṭ tom tom ta)

The gap in this case is the three-pulse *$tām_3$*

g = 3, [$tām_3$]

The mōrā, then, is (6) [3] (6) [3] (6), or twenty-four pulses.

Remember that the mōrā must *end* the cycle, which is thirty-two pulses long. This means that eight pulses must be inserted before the mōrā. We can use phrase *a* as stage IV:

{a} + (ta ta kṭ tom tom ta) [$tām_3$] (ta ta kṭ tom tom ta) [$tām_3$] (ta ta kṭ tom tom ta) **(06-072)**

Here is the full composition, including the first mōrā.

Ādi Mōrā 1 **(06-073N)**

STAGE I
{abcd abce}, twice

STAGE II
{abce}, twice

STAGE III
{aebecede}

STAGE IV
{a}

ĀDI MŌRĀ 1
(ta ta kṭ tom tom ta) [$tām_3$] (ta ta kṭ tom tom ta) [$tām_3$] (ta ta kṭ tom tom ta)

Variations on the First Mōrā: Breaking Another Rule

In tiśra jāti ēka mōrā series 1, examples 5 and 6 contained more than three statements and two gaps. The justification we used was that the expansion and contraction were orderly and exhaustive. The variations on the first ādi tāḷa mōrā are not entirely orderly in their contraction or expansion yet are generally considered aesthetically justifiable. Here is variation 1.

Variation 1: Ādi Mōrā 2 **(06-074)**

s_1(ta ta kṭ tom tom ta) [$tām_2$] 6 + 2
s_2(kṭ tom tom ta) [$tām_2$] 4 + 2
s_3(tom tom ta) [$tām_2$] 3 + 2
s_4(tom ta) [$tām_2$] 2 + 2
s_5(ta) 1

The total is still twenty-four pulses (with the gaps reduced to g = 2), and it is exhaustive. There are five statements. The reduction from statement 1 to statement 2 is two pulses, while statement 2 through statement 5 reduce one pulse at a time, from four pulses, to three, to two, and to one. Notice that from statement 2 on, variation 1 is rhythmically identical to mōrā 5 in tiśra jāti ēka mōrā series 1:

(ta ka din ta) [$tām_2$] 4 + 2
(ka din ta) [$tām_2$] 3 + 2
(din ta) [$tām_2$] 2 + 2
(ta) 1

Variation 2 uses the same process we applied in series 1, mōrā 6. It simply reverses the order of the statements, expanding rather than contracting them.

Variation 2: Ādi Mōrā 3 **(06-075)**

(ta) [$tām_2$] 1 + 2
(tom ta) [$tām_2$] 2 + 2
(tom tom ta) [$tām_2$] 3 + 2
(kṭ tom tom ta) [$tām_2$] 4 + 2
(ta ta kṭ tom tom ta) 6

Here is the full composition, using variation 1: **(06-076N)**

STAGE I
{abcd abce}, twice

STAGE II
{abce}, twice

STAGE III
{aebecede}

STAGE IV
{a}

ĀDI MŌRĀ 2
(ta ta kṭ tom tom ta) [$tām_2$] 6 + 2
(kṭ tom tom ta) [$tām_2$] 4 + 2
(tom tom ta) [$tām_2$] 3 + 2
(tom ta) [$tām_2$] 2 + 2
(ta) 1

Here is the full composition, using variation 2: **(06-077N)**

STAGE I
{abcd abce}, twice

STAGE II
{abce}, twice

STAGE III
{aebecede}

STAGE IV

{a}

ĀDI MŌRĀ 3

(ta) [tām_2] 1 + 2

(tom ta) [tām_2] 2 + 2

(tom tom ta) [tām_2] 3 + 2

(kṭ tom tom ta) [tām_2] 4 + 2

(ta ta kṭ tom tom ta) 6

The three versions may be performed in sequence, returning to stage III each time.

The first discussion of the mōrā form characterized it as *fractal,* meaning that its logic should remain constant at simple and complex levels of scale. An example of this fractal logic is the *compound* mōrā. A mōrā may be performed three times in succession without returning to a sarvalaghu figure after each one. In this case, each performance becomes a statement in a compound mōrā, with a gap of zero. Look at the following examples, using the twenty-four-pulse mōrā above and its variations:

Compound Mōrā 1 **(06-078N)**

((ta ta kṭ tom tom ta) [tām_3] (ta ta kṭ tom tom ta) [tām_3] (ta ta kṭ tom tom ta))
((ta ta kṭ tom tom ta) [tām_3] (ta ta kṭ tom tom ta) [tām_3] (ta ta kṭ tom tom ta))
((ta ta kṭ tom tom ta) [tām_3] (ta ta kṭ tom tom ta) [tām_3] (ta ta kṭ tom tom ta))

Compound Mōrā 2 **(06-079N)**

((ta ta kṭ tom tom ta) [tām_2]
(kṭ tom tom ta) [tām_2]
(tom tom ta) [tām_2]
(tom ta) [tām_2]
(ta))
((ta ta kṭ tom tom ta) [tām_2]
(kṭ tom tom ta) [tām_2]
(tom tom ta) [tām_2]
(tom ta) [tām_2]
(ta))
((ta ta kṭ tom tom ta) [tām_2]
(kṭ tom tom ta) [tām_2]
(tom tom ta) [tām_2]
(tom ta) [tām_2]
(ta))

Compound Mōrā 3 **(06-080N)**

((ta) [tām_2]
(tom ta) [tām_2]
(tom tom ta) [tām_2]
(kṭ tom tom ta) [tām_2]
(ta ta kṭ tom tom ta))
((ta) [tām_2]
(tom ta) [tām_2]
(tom tom ta) [tām_2]
(kṭ tom tom ta) [tām_2]
(ta ta kṭ tom tom ta))
((ta) [tām_2]
(tom ta) [tām_2]
(tom tom ta) [tām_2]
(kṭ tom tom ta) [tām_2]
(ta ta kṭ tom tom ta))

The arrangement of phrases in a mōrā may be expressed as a rhythmic "shape." Rhythmic shapes in Karnatak music are referred to as *yati*. Six of these are recognized, of which we will discuss five (the last shape, *viśama* is actually a catchall meaning "not the same" and is used to describe phrases that do not comprise an orderly design).

Three of these are simple: sama, gopucca, and srotovaha. *Sama* refers to figures in which the phrases are all the same (for example, mōrā 1 above). *Gopucca* (cow's tail) refers to figures in which the phrases go from longer to shorter (for example, variation 1). *Srotovaha* (river mouth) refers to figures in which the phrases go from shorter to longer (for example, variation 2).

Each of the compound mōrā examples so far keeps to one of these three simple shapes. Compound mōrā 1 is an example of *sama* yati in all of its statements; compound mōrā 2 exemplifies three sets of *gopucca* yati statements; and compound mōrā 3 exemplifies three sets of *srotovaha* yati statements.

Two shapes are compound: *mṛdaṅga* and *damaru. Damaru,* named for the hourglass-shaped drum played by the Hindu god Śiva, refers to figures in which the phrases go from longer to shorter and back to longer. *Mṛdaṅga,* named after the barrel-shaped drum used throughout Karnatak music, represents the reverse, shorter to longer to shorter.

Mixing the statements results in examples of these compound yatis. For example, if we string together variation 1 (gopucca), mōrā 1 (sama), and variation 2 (srotovaha), the resulting compound mōrā is an example of *damaru yati.*

Compound Mōrā 4 **(06-081N)**

((ta ta kṭ tom tom ta) [tām_2]
(kṭ tom tom ta) [tām_2]

(tom tom ta) [tām_2]
(tom ta) [tām_2]
(ta))
((ta ta kṭ tom tom ta) [tām_3]
(ta ta kṭ tom tom ta) [tām_3]
(ta ta kṭ tom tom ta))
((ta) [tām_2]
(tom ta) [tām_2]
(tom tom ta) [tām_2]
(kṭ tom tom ta) [tām_2]
(ta ta kṭ tom tom ta))

If we reverse the order, beginning with variation 2 (srotovaha), adding mōrā 1 (sama), and ending with variation 1 (gopucca), the result is an example of *mṛdaṅga yati*.

Compound Mōrā 5 **(06-082)**

((ta) [tām_2]
(tom ta) [tām_2]
(tom tom ta) [tām_2]
(kṭ tom tom ta) [tām_2]
(ta ta kṭ tom tom ta))
((ta ta kṭ tom tom ta) [tām_3]
(ta ta kṭ tom tom ta) [tām_3]
(ta ta kṭ tom tom ta))
((ta ta kṭ tom tom ta) [tām_2]
(kṭ tom tom ta) [tām_2]
(tom tom ta) [tām_2]
(tom ta) [tām_2]
(ta))

In order to use any of the compound mōrās, we need to alter stage IV of the setup, because each compound mōrā totals seventy-two pulses. The nearest multiple of thirty-two is ninety-six, three cycles of the tāḷa. Stage IV, then, must comprise twenty-four pulses. This total is neatly arrived at by using the figure *{aeb}*.

The new composition, altered for the compound mōrās, now looks like this:

STAGE I
{abcd abce}, twice

STAGE II
{abce}, twice

STAGE III

{aebecede}

STAGE IV

{aeb}

Any of the five compound mōrās

PERFORMANCE STRATEGY

When done by an ensemble, stages I through IV can be performed by the entire group, with the compound mōrās performed as solos. Repeat back to stage IV after each solo. Here is a suggested sequence: **(06-083AV)**

STAGE I

{abcd abce}, twice

STAGE II

{abce}, twice

STAGE III

{aebecede}

STAGE IV

{aeb}

Compound mōrā 4 **(06-081N)**

STAGE IV

{aeb}

Compound mōrā 1 **(06-078N)**

STAGE IV

{aeb}

Compound mōrā 5 **(06-082N)**

It is customary to draw such an elaborate section to a close with a small mōrā called *arudi*. It is brief, taking a cycle or less, and is often related to the material that preceded it.

Our arudi will maintain the same structure as the original twenty-four pulse mōrā, namely s = 6, g = 3, but in a more densely articulated form. The phrase *(ta ta kṭ tom tom ta)* becomes *(tk tr kṭ tom tom ta)*, in which *tk tr kṭ* is a double-speed abbreviation for *ta ka ta ri ki ṭa*. The phrase [tām_3] becomes [tām kṭ tk]. The full arudi, then, is

(tk tr kṭ tom tom ta) [tām kṭ tk] (tk tr kṭ tom tom ta) [tām kṭ tk] (tk tr kṭ tom tom ta) **(06-084)**

It begins eight pulses after the beginning of the cycle, at the same point as the original twenty-four pulse mōrā.

$\textbf{tām}_8$
(tk tr kṭ tom tom ta) [tām kṭ tk]
(tk tr kṭ tom tom ta) [tām kṭ tk]
(tk tr kṭ tom tom ta) **tām**

In this case, the final tām will be the first syllable in the next section.

Notice the dense articulations in the gap of the arudi. As you practice this arudi, you are likely to notice that these articulations at the end of the gap have the effect of blurring the boundary between the gap and the beginning of the next statement, which *begins* with dense articulations. This sort of concealment of boundaries is an important aesthetic device in Karnatak music; it will surface at other points in the following lessons.

GLOSSARY

arudi (ah-ru-dee): A brief mōrā used to mark important structural points in a tani āvartanam.

yati (yuh-tea): Rhythmic shape.

sama yati (sah-mah yuh-tea): A group of phrases that are all the same duration.

gopucca yati (go-put-cha yuh-tea): A group of phrases that get progressively shorter.

srotovaha yati (shro-toe-vah-hah yuh-tea): A group of phrases that get progressively longer.

damaru yati (dah-mah-roo yuh-tea): A group of phrases that get progressively shorter, then longer.

mṛdaṅga yati (mri-dun-gah yuh-tea): A group of phrases that get progressively longer, then shorter.

viśama yati (vih-sha-mah yuh-tea): A group of phrases with no regular shape.

7 · A COMPOSITION BY PALANI SRI M. SUBRAMANIA PILLAI (1908–1962)

This section introduces a rhythmic *composition*. This is not a composition in the European sense, in that it was never transmitted in writing. Still, the notion of composition raises the issue of attribution. If we call it a composition, who composed it? Much of the material South Indian drummers play is in the public domain, but there are some pieces of rhythmic material that can be attributed to one person or another.

What constitutes a composition? In many cases it will be a mōrā or kōrvai, introduced by a particular musician, that for one reason or another has become popular or influential. In this case it refers to a set-up and mōrā that have entered the mainstream along with their attribution to Palani Sri M. Subramania Pillai. We will refer to this great master as Sri Palani.

Sri Palani's fame as a composer is partly due to his skill at upsetting expectations by performing material that was designed to fit comfortably in one metric setting in a contrasting, much less comfortable setting. He particularly favored playing patterns grouped in sets of four in other pulse groupings, such as three pulses per beat.

Mōrās and kōrvais, which can happen nearly anywhere in a tani, are mostly independent of the preceding sarvalaghu; nearly any kōrvai can be played with any sarvalaghu. Some of Sri Palani's compositions form a new type, consisting of a set of sarvalaghu phrases and a mōrā designed to be played as a unit. The sarvalaghu/mōrā unit may be played several times in shifting pulse groupings.

What we are calling a composition will not be literally what Sri Palani played, nor need it be. In the spirit of Karnatak drumming, improvisation and alteration begin almost as soon as any composition is learned. In fact, this particular compositional idea has inspired many other drummers' creations.

What remains is its set of essential features, in this case a six-cycle composition designed to be played or spoken in different pulse groupings, including *tiśra naḍai* (three, six, or twelve pulses per beat).

Tiśra Naḍai and the Notion of "Triplets" in European Music

The phrases *a, b, c,* and *d* shown below are all designed to fit comfortably into groups of two or four beats at four pulses per beat. When we change to three- or six-pulse divisions, a process known as tiśra naḍai, we do so over a constant tāḷa. This means that the rate of the pulses slows down from four to three, or speeds up from four to six, within each regular beat. The phrases, however, retain their quadruple shapes and accents; they therefore generate tension with the three- or six-pulse beats.

Tiśra naḍai, then, is not quite the same as the *triplet* in European music, where the phrases take on the shape of the three-pulse beat, *one* two three, *one* two three, and so on. In order to speak or play comfortably in tiśra naḍai, we need to be able to feel the entire *cycle* as it is divided into thirds.

The Thirds of the Cycle and How to Find Them

The following exercise provides the physical, or kinesthetic, experience of shifting from two, to three, and then to four syllables per beat using a pattern grouped into fours. **(07-085N)**

Use the pattern *ta ka di mi ta ka jo ṇu.*
Speak this pattern twice in one cycle, at two syllables per beat.

|| **ta** ka | di mi | ta ka | jo ṇu | **ta** ka | di mi | ta ka | jo ṇu ||

Increase the speed to three pulses per beat, resulting in three patterns per cycle.

|| **ta** ka di | mi ta ka | jo ṇu **ta** | ka di mi | ta ka jo | ṇu **ta** ka | di mi ta | ka jo ṇu ||

Increase the speed to four pulses per beat, resulting in four patterns per cycle.

|| **ta** ka di mi | ta ka jo ṇu | **ta** ka di mi | ta ka jo ṇu
| **ta** ka di mi |ta ka jo ṇu |**ta** ka di mi |ta ka jo ṇu ||

Speak the entire pattern four times, and practice until the changes are comfortable.

Notice that the first and third versions, two and four patterns per cycle, fit very comfortably in the tāḷa, but that the second one does not. Each pattern in this example takes two and two-thirds beats, or one third of a cycle. The phrases *a, b, c,* and *d* below may be thought of as double-time equivalents of the simple *ta ka di mi ta ka jo nu*. It may be helpful to substitute each of these in turn for the simple exercise phrase in order to become conversant with the way these phrases fit within the tāḷa.

Here are the phrases. Note that the phrase *tr gḍ* in lines *a* and *c* is a double-speed abbreviation for *ta ri gi ḍu*, and that the phrase *kṭ tk* in line *d* and in the mōrā is an abbreviated version of *ki ṭa ta ka*. Simplify the phrases in the six-per-beat and double-speed versions, since "tr gḍ" and "din na kṭ tk" may be difficult to say at these rates. This sort of substitution is common among drummers, who routinely simplify fingerings at faster speeds. Substitute "ki ṭa" for "tr gḍ" and "ta ka jo ṇu" for "din na kṭ tk," as follows:

a. original speed: tām_4 ta ka din_2 din_2 din_2 na_2 **tr gḍ (07-086)**

   six-per-beat and double speed: tām_4 ta ka din_2 din_2 din_2 na_2 **ki ṭa**

b. original speed: tom ta ka tom ta ka din_2 tām_2 tām_2 dī_4 **(07-087)**

   six-per-beat and double speed: tom ta ka tom ta ka din_2 tām_2 tām_2 dī_4

c. original speed: • • ki ṭa ta ka din_2 din_2 din_2 na_2 **tr gḍ (07–088)**

six-per-beat and double speed: • • ki ṭa ta ka din_2 din_2 din_2 na_2 **ki ṭa**

d. original speed: tom ta ka tom ta ka din_2 **din na kṭ tk** $tām_4$ **(07-089)**

six-per-beat and double speed: tom ta ka tom ta ka din_2 **ta ka jo ṇu** $tām_4$

Once you are familiar with these phrases, practice the composition's mōrā on its own. Here are the phrases for the original version:

mōrā: s = 20, ($tām_4$ ta ka di na tom ta ka tom ta ka di na **din na kṭ tk**), g = 2 [$tām_2$] **(07-090)**

And here are the phrases for six-per-beat and double-speed:

mōrā: s = 20, ($tām_4$ ta ka di na tom ta ka tom ta ka di na **ta ka jo ṇu**), g = 2 [$tām_2$]

Here is the form of the entire composition:

{abcd} ∗ 2 + mōrā

Note that the whole composition takes six cycles at four pulses per beat. It can be performed thrice, without interruption, each time in a different pulse grouping.

First, recite it at the original setting, four pulses per beat. At this speed it takes six cycles.

Next, increase the speed by half, from four to six pulses per beat. At this speed it takes four cycles.

Third, double the original speed to eight pulses per beat. At this speed it takes three cycles. **(07-091N)**

Notice that the notation, especially at the fastest speed, requires a great deal of abbreviation in order to fit within the beats. Remember that the notation is only an aid and is not intended to be read in the same way as Western music notation. By the time you have memorized the composition, the notation should not even be necessary. Keep in mind that the syllables for six-per-beat and double-speed are identical.

This completes the composition by Sri Palani. Before going on to the next section, finish the composition with the same arudi that completed ādi tāḷa mōrā series 1:

$tām_8$ (tk tr kṭ tom tom ta) [tām kṭ tk] (tk tr kṭ tom tom ta) [tām kṭ tk] (tk tr kṭ tom tom ta)

GLOSSARY

tiśra naḍai (tish-ra na-dye): Division of the beat into three, six, or twelve notes.

8 · A KŌRVAI WITH ITS SETUP

This section introduces another type of design, called *kōrvai*. The kōrvai form is more elaborate than the mōrā and more sparingly used. It is almost always pre-composed and designed to fit a particular tāḷa setting.

The kōrvai seldom occurs in tasteful accompaniment, whereas small mōrās may be used as seasoning throughout a song. Its most frequent use is in the tani āvartanam, where it marks important structural points. Every tani must contain at least one kōrvai, at its end, but most tanis contain several. How many of these appear in a solo depends on time, among other factors.

Though a particular kōrvai might have been composed so that its pulse total matches that of a specific tāḷa, its internal phrase structure is likely to generate significant tension with the tāḷa; it may be quite difficult to perform precisely. A kōrvai therefore may require a great deal of practice; each one must be mastered in all of its possible manifestations.

The kōrvai form is quite flexible, with only two firm rules. First, it must have at least two parts, though it may have several. These sections generally express some type of rhythmic shape, or *yati*. The other firm rule is that its final section must be a mōrā.

Following the pattern we have already established, we introduce phrases from a kōrvai by means of sarvalaghu figures. The particular sarvalaghu pattern that sets up a kōrvai is discretionary, depending on the part of the solo in which the kōrvai is introduced. It is generally possible to use any kōrvai at any stage of a tani.

As was the case with ādi tāḷa mōrā, series 1, the introductory phrase first appears at the end of one or more cycles of sarvalaghu. It then appears at increasingly frequent intervals, for example, at one-cycle, half-cycle, and quarter-cycle intervals, so that the time-reinforcing character of the sarvalaghu is maintained.

When the kōrvai is finally stated, it is customarily done either once or three times. A long, elaborate kōrvai may be done only once. If it is done three times, the second and third times will almost certainly include variations.

This particular kōrvai, again attributed to Sri Palani, is built entirely from a single twenty-one pulse phrase. Here it is, in a simplified version:

ta ki ṭa tom_2 ta din gi ṇa tom jo ṇu jo ṇu tom_2 ta_2 tām_3 **(08-092)**

The kōrvai develops by repeating, then cutting off, parts of the phrase, as follows:

ta ki ṭa tom_2 ta din gi ṇa tom jo ṇu jo ṇu tom_2 ta_2 $tām_3$
ta ki ṭa tom_2 ta din gi ṇa tom jo ṇu jo ṇu tom_2 ta_2 $tām_3$
ta ki ṭa tom_2 ta din gi ṇa tom jo ṇu jo ṇu tom_2 ta_2 $tām_3$
jo ṇu jo ṇu tom_2 ta_2 $tām_3$
jo ṇu jo ṇu tom_2 ta_2 $tām_3$
tom_2 ta_2 $tām_3$
tom_2 ta_2 **(08-093)**

If we represent the kōrvai in this way, the rhythmic shape is clear enough; the phrases get shorter each time. But where is the mōrā?

This kōrvai's structure is somewhat subtle and requires some analysis. We can break it into sections:

a. ta ki ṭa tom_2 ta din gi ṇa tom = ten pulses
b. jo ṇu jo ṇu = four pulses
c. tom_2 ta_2 = four pulses
d. $tām_3$ = three pulses

We can represent the sequence as follows:

abcd 10 + 4 + 4 + 3 = 21
abcd 10 + 4 + 4 + 3 = 21
abcd 10 + 4 + 4 + 3 = 21
bcd 4 + 4 + 3 = 11
b (c) [d] 4 + (4) + [3] = 11
(c) [d] (4) + [3] = 7
(c) (4), 96 pulses total

This representation shows that the rules of structure are intact. The first sections express a non-arithmetical gopucca yati, while the mōrā is (c) [d] (c) [d] (c).

The kōrvai's ninety-six pulses require three full cycles of ādi tāḷa. This total suggests that the kōrvai could be used both in ādi tāḷa and in any tāḷa of three, six, or twelve beats. Since this is the middle of the solo, we will set up the kōrvai with a middle-tempo sarvalaghu pattern, one that has a syllable for each of the four pulses in the beat. Here are the phrases:

a. din_2 ta na ta ta jo ṇu
b. jo ṇu ta na ta ta jo ṇu
c. din_2 ta ta jo ṇu
d. jo ṇu ta ta jo ṇu

Kōrvai 1 with Setup **(08-094N)**

STAGE I
abbb abc + ta ki ṭa tom_2 ta din gi ṇa tom (two cycles)
abbb abd + ta ki ṭa tom_2 ta din gi ṇa tom (two cycles)

STAGE II

abc + ta ki ṭa tom_2 ta din gi ṇa tom (one cycle)

abd + ta ki ṭa tom_2 ta din gi ṇa tom (one cycle)

STAGE III

c + phrase (half cycle)

d + phrase (half cycle)

Kōrvai, one time only

There are several possible variations on this kōrvai. The first variations focus on the mōrā. The mōrā statements, as we have seen, do not have to be equal but should increase or decrease by equal increments. In this case, the statements increase or decrease by two pulses each time.

This is the original mōrā:

(tom_2 ta_2) [tām_3] (tom_2 ta_2) [tām_3] (tom_2 ta_2)

VARIATION 1 **(08-095N)**

(tom ta) [tām_3] (tom_2 ta_2) [tām_3] (tom_3 ta_3)

VARIATION 2 **(08-096N)**

(tom_3 ta_3) [tām_3] (tom_2 ta_2) [tām_3] (tom ta)

The second variations focus on phrase *c*. In the sequence outline above, note that the *c* figure, tom_2 ta_2, occurs seven times, for a total of twenty-eight pulses. If we let c^2 = tom ta, c^4 = tom_2 ta_2, and c^6 = tom_3 ta_3, where the superscript numbers indicate the number of pulses, we can vary them as follows in the sequence without disturbing the total number of pulses:

VARIATION 3 **(08-097N)**

abc^2d

abc^4d

abc^6d

bc^4d

bc^2d

c^4d

c^6

The reverse is also possible:

VARIATION 4 **(08-098N)**

abc^6d

abc^4d

abc^2d

bc^4d

bc^6d

c^4d

c^2

While none of these variations changes the pulse total, each results in a significantly different rhythmic effect. Now there are five versions, the original and four variations.

This kōrvai may be performed just once, as in the example above, or it may be performed three times by making use of the variations. Here are two suggestions for doing it three times.

1. original + variation 1 + variation 2
2. original + variation 3 + variation 4

The simplified version used so far shows the structure of the kōrvai in a very clear manner. T. Ranganathan, a student of Sri Palani, devised it for a kanjira student. The original version, which contains double-time patterns, was too difficult to play with one hand. In the original phrases, shown below, the phrase *tr gg tr gḍ dk tk tr gḍ* is an abbreviated form of *ta ri gu gu ta ri gi ḍu di ku ta ka ta ri gi ḍu,* and the phrase *tr gḍ* is an abbreviated form of *ta ri gi ḍu.*

a. ta_2 tr gg tr gḍ dk tk tr gḍ
b. tr gḍ ta_2
c. tom_2 ta_2
d. $tām_3$

This will almost certainly be difficult to pronounce; the sixteen note phrase *ta ri gu gu ta ri gi ḍu di ku ta ka ta ri gi ḍu* should be isolated and practiced separately as follows:

Following the pattern established in the first *trikāla* exercise, speak the pattern in three speeds, so that each speed uses a full cycle of the tāḷa. Do two cycles of each: **(08-099)**

ta_2 ri_2 gu_2 gu_2 ta_2 ri_2 gi_2 $ḍu_2$ di_2 ku_2 ta_2 ka_2 ta_2 ri_2 gi_2 $ḍu_2$ $* 2$
ta ri gu gu ta ri gi ḍu di ku ta ka ta ri gi ḍu $* 4$
tr gg tr gḍ dk tk tr gḍ $* 8$

Using only the faster two speeds, divide the pattern into two groups of eight:

a. ta ri gu gu ta ri gi ḍu
b. di ku ta ka ta ri gi ḍu

Recite the following patterns many times each: **(08-100)**

ababaaab
abababbb

This version of the kōrvai conceals the structure in a way that the simplified version does not. The ear is likely to hear it this way:

ta_2 tr gg tr gḍ dk tk tr gḍ tr gḍ
ta_2 tom_2 ta_2
$tām_3$

Concealment of this kind is another distinguishing feature of Sri Palani's material. We have already experienced it in the arudi we use at the ends of sections.

Practice the kōrvai again, using the filled-out version. All of the variations involving "c" will still be in order. There are now ten versions of this kōrvai. **(08-101N–08-105N)**

As we said at the beginning of this section, a kōrvai is typically performed once or three times. Under some circumstances, a kōrvai may be played twice, but only if there is a significant difference in treatment from one performance to the next. This kind of treatment is not considered to be doing the kōrvai twice but rather "once and once."

Since the next section of the tani is set in tiśra naḍai, or three pulses per beat, we can use this kōrvai as a bridge, or transition, into that pulse grouping. Here are two ways to do this. The first makes use of the simplified version; the second, the original filled-out version.

> Simplified version: once at four pulses per beat, once at six pulses per beat (five cycles total) **(tani for one player)**

> Original version: once at four pulses per beat, once at *three* pulses per beat (seven cycles total) **(tani for two players)**

There are practical and aesthetic considerations associated with both transitions. In the first, the syllables are sparsely articulated, so it is possible to speed up to six syllables per beat, making a lively transition. In the second, the patterns are already at double speed; it would be quite difficult to speed up from eight to twelve syllables per beat. In this case, dropping from eight to six syllables per beat creates an effective transition.

This transition leaves out the arudi, going directly from the tiśra naḍai kōrvai into the tiśra naḍai sarvalaghu that sets up the next kōrvai. It is also possible to perform three versions of the kōrvai at four pulses per beat, follow it with the standard arudi, and begin the tiśra naḍai sarvalaghu that opens the next section without warning. Practice it both ways.

9 · TIŚRA NAḌAI, SARVALAGHU AND KŌRVAI

It is customary to perform a section of a tani entirely in a pulse grouping (*naḍai*) that contrasts with the grouping in which the solo began. Any kaṇakku designs, along with the sarvalaghu figures used to set them up, will reflect this contrasting pulse grouping. Because the original setting for our tani is ādi tāḷa at four pulses per beat (*caturaśra naḍai*), or thirty-two per cycle, we will do a brief section in *tiśra* naḍai, meaning that patterns and designs will move at three, six, or twelve syllables per beat.

The sarvalaghu and kōrvai in this section move at three pulses per beat. We will use the same pattern we introduced in the tiśra jāti ēka tāḷa lessons, *din*$_2$ *ta ta din*$_2$ (pattern *a* below), with two variations, labeled *b* and *c*.

a. din$_2$ ta ta din$_2$
b. • • ta ta din$_2$
c. ta na ta ta din$_2$

The kōrvai is based on the following twelve-pulse phrase, also with two variations:

i. ta di$_2$ ta tom$_3$ ta di ki ṭa tom
ii. • di$_2$ ta tom$_3$ ta di ki ṭa tom
iii. • • • ta tom$_3$ ta di ki ṭa tom

Note that the phrase *ta di ki ṭa tom* is a variant of *ta din gi ṇa tom*. These phrases may be used interchangeably but should be kept consistent within one composition or kōrvai. Because the kōrvai in the previous section made use of *ta din gi ṇa tom,* we will use *ta di ki ṭa tom* in this section.

Here is the entire composition, beginning with the sarvalaghu setup. **(09-106N)**

Stage I, two cycles for each line
a b a c a b + i
a b a c a b + ii
a b a c a b + iii

Stage II, one cycle for each line
a b + i
a b + ii
a b + iii

Stage III, one half cycle for each line. Do this whole section twice.
i ii iii

KŌRVAI

The first part of the kōrvai is made up of the lines i, ii, and iii, *but without the silent pulses at the beginnings of lines ii and iii.* Instead of each line totaling twelve pulses, the total gets smaller each time, as follows:

ta di_2 ta tom_3 ta di ki ṭa tom = 12 pulses
di_2 ta tom_3 ta di ki ṭa tom = 11 pulses
ta tom_3 ta di ki ṭa tom = 9 pulses

Two more structural details contribute to this kōrvai. First, a three-pulse *$tām_3$* is added to each of the first two lines:

ta di_2 ta tom_3 ta di ki ṭa tom *$tām_3$* [12 + 3 = 15 pulses]
di_2 ta tom_3 ta di ki ṭa tom *$tām_3$* [11 + 3 = 14 pulses]

Next, the phrase *ta di ki ṭa tom* at the end of the third line has a double function as the first statement in its mōrā:

ta tom_3 *(ta di ki ṭa tom) (ta di ki ṭa tom) (ta di ki ṭa tom)*

The clearest notation of this kōrvai shows these additions and double functions in italics. Note that it separates the mōrā; this separation will make the following exploration of possible variations easier to understand. Its pulse total is now forty-eight: two cycles of ādi tāḷa at three pulses per beat, or twenty-four per cycle.

ta di_2 ta tom_3 ta di ki ṭa tom *$tām_3$* [12 + 3 = 15 pulses]
di_2 ta tom_3 ta di ki ṭa tom *$tām_3$* [11 + 3 = 14 pulses]
ta tom_3 = 4 pulses
(ta di ki ṭa tom) (ta di ki ṭa tom) (ta di ki ṭa tom) = 15 pulses, 48 total

Realization 1

The simplest possible realization of the kōrvai is to perform it three times as given. Do this before trying the variations.

TIŚRA KŌRVAI 1: ORIGINAL VERSION **(09-107N)**
ta di_2 ta tom_3 ta di ki ṭa tom $tām_3$ = 15 pulses
di_2 ta tom_3 ta di ki ṭa tom $tām_3$ = 14 pulses
ta tom_3 = 4 pulses
(ta di ki ṭa tom) (ta di ki ṭa tom) (ta di ki ṭa tom) = 15 pulses

This kōrvai's structure suggests three variations and an alternate version with its own three variations. Note the figure *tām₃* that ends each of the first two lines. Because there are two of these, they can move into the kōrvai's mōrā as the two gaps.

VARIATION 1 **(09-108N)**
ta di_2 ta tom_3 ta di ki ṭa tom = 12 pulses
di_2 ta tom_3 ta di ki ṭa tom = 11 pulses
ta tom_3 = 4 pulses
(ta di ki ṭa tom) [*$tām_3$*] (ta di ki ṭa tom) [*$tām_3$*] (ta di ki ṭa tom) = 21 pulses

It is not necessary for all three pulses in each *tām* to be either at the end of the first two lines or to function as gaps in the mōrā. They can also be distributed in two other ways, as variations 2 and 3 will show.

VARIATION 2 **(09-109N)**
In this variation each of the first two lines ends with a two-pulse *tām,* with the remaining pulse becoming the mōrā gap.

ta di_2 ta tom_3 ta di ki ṭa tom *$tām_2$* = 14 pulses
di_2 ta tom_3 ta di ki ṭa tom *$tām_2$* = 13 pulses
ta tom_3 = 4 pulses
(ta di ki ṭa tom) [•] (ta di ki ṭa tom) [•] (ta di ki ṭa tom) = 17 pulses

VARIATION 3 **(09-110N)**
For variation 3 we simply reverse this process, leaving one pulse at the end of each of the first two lines and using the two-pulse *tām* as the mōrā gap.

ta di_2 ta tom_3 ta di ki ṭa tom • = 13 pulses
di_2 ta tom_3 ta di ki ṭa tom • = 12 pulses
ta tom_3 = 4 pulses
(ta di ki ṭa tom) [*$tām_2$*] (ta di ki ṭa tom) [*$tām_2$*] (ta di ki ṭa tom) = 19 pulses

Practice Tip: Drill the variations in sets of three. Since we are redistributing the spaces, the phrases of the kōrvai variations will fit differently in the tāḷa than they do in the original version. They are likely to be challenging. Practice them in sets of three in order to get accustomed to the differences in the tāḷa-kōrvai relationship.

An alternate version of this kōrvai leaves the three-pulse *tām* unarticulated. In this alternate version and its variations, note that the pulse totals are the same as those of the original and its corresponding variations.

KŌRVAI: ALTERNATE VERSION **(09-111N)**
ta di_2 ta tom_3 ta di ki ṭa tom $•_3$ = 15 pulses
di_2 ta tom_3 ta di ki ṭa tom $•_3$ = 14 pulses

ta tom_3 = 4 pulses
(ta di ki ṭa tom) (ta di ki ṭa tom) (ta di ki ṭa tom) = 15 pulses

Variations 4, 5, and 6 parallel variations 1, 2, and 3, except that the syllable *tām* is replaced by an unsounded pulse. Thus *$tām_3$* becomes $\bullet_3$, and *$tām_2$* becomes $\bullet_2$.

VARIATION 4 **(09-112N)**
ta di_2 ta tom_3 ta di ki ṭa tom = 12 pulses
di_2 ta tom_3 ta di ki ṭa tom = 11 pulses
ta tom_3 = 4 pulses
(ta di ki ṭa tom) [$\bullet_3$] (ta di ki ṭa tom) [$\bullet_3$] (ta di ki ṭa tom) = 21 pulses

VARIATION 5 **(09-113N)**
ta di_2 ta tom_3 ta di ki ṭa tom $\bullet_2$ = 14 pulses
di_2 ta tom_3 ta di ki ṭa tom $\bullet_2$ = 13 pulses
ta tom_3 = 4 pulses
(ta di ki ṭa tom) [•] (ta di ki ṭa tom) [•] (ta di ki ṭa tom) = 17 pulses

VARIATION 6 **(09-114N)**
ta di_2 ta tom_3 ta di ki ṭa tom • = 13 pulses
di_2 ta tom_3 ta di ki ṭa tom • = 12 pulses
ta tom_3 = 4 pulses
(ta di ki ṭa tom) [$\bullet_2$] (ta di ki ṭa tom) [$\bullet_2$] (ta di ki ṭa tom) = 19 pulses

While there is no hard and fast rule about which variations to perform or in what sequence, the following realizations provide the most orderly development through three statements of the kōrvai.

Realization 2 **(09-115) (09-107N, 09-109N, 09-110N)**

original version
variation 2
variation 3

Realization 3 **(09-116) (09-111N, 09-113N, 09-114N)**

alternate version
variation 5
variation 6

A typical tani might include other setups and kaṇakku designs in a contrasting naḍai such as this one, or it might, as we are about to do, return to the original pulse grouping. Use the same arudi we have employed so far, again at four pulses per beat:

$tām_8$ (tk tr kṭ tom tom ta) [tām kṭ tk] (tk tr kṭ tom tom ta) [tām kṭ tk] (tk tr kṭ tom tom ta) **tām**

10 · MIŚRA KORAIPPU

A tani āvartanam may be performed by a solo artist or by a group of musicians. Since this material is designed for a group, we may make use of a device called *koraippu*, which means "to reduce." This falls under the heading of kaṇakku but has a more improvisatory character than the mōrās and kōrvais we have seen to this point.

Koraippu is a section in which performers trade phrases in progressively smaller groups until everyone is playing together. Jazz musicians also trade groups of measures: eight measures, then four, then two, and so on. Trading in jazz often follows the song form, which is contained by a set number of measures according to a given song's harmonic structure, for example twelve, sixteen, or thirty-two measures.

Since Karnatak music song forms are open ended, not bounded by a harmonic structure, trading must be organized another way. Karnatak musicians often organize a koraippu according to numbers of tāḷa cycles: two cycles, then single cycles, then half cycles and quarter cycles. In such a koraippu the players are free to play whatever phrases and small designs come to mind within each segment of the tāḷa.

A more elaborately organized approach to trading is based on rhythmic phrases that generate tension with the tāḷa setting. For example, a group of musicians playing in the eight-beat ādi tāḷa might trade groups of seven-note phrases. In a seven-beat cycle they might trade phrases of six notes each, while in a five-beat cycle they could trade nine-note phrases. For our purposes, the first example, seven-note phrases in ādi tāḷa, will work perfectly. Our koraippu will go through four stages of trading before the performers come together in unison. In stage I we will trade two-cycle groups (sixteen beats), in stage II single cycles (eight beats), in stage III half cycles (four beats), and in stage IV quarter cycles (two beats).

Koraippu Stage I

This will employ eight seven-note phrases, or fifty-six pulses, eight fewer than the sixty-four pulses in two cycles of ādi tāḷa. These eight pulses, articulated by a single *tām*, will be counted silently at the beginning of the first cycle and occupy two beats. The eight seven-note phrases thus begin on the third beat of the first cycle. We can think of this as a formula: $8*1 + 8*7 = 64$.

STAGE I, PATTERN 1 **(10-117N)**

tām$_8$ **ta** ka di mi ta ki ṭa **ta** ka di mi ta ki ṭa **ta** ka di mi ta ki ṭa **ta** ka di mi ta ki ṭa
ta ka di mi ta ki ṭa **ta** ka di mi ta ki ṭa **ta** ka di mi ta ki ṭa **ta** ka di mi ta ki ṭa

Once the koraippu context (tāḷa and contrasting phrase grouping) is set, the sevens can become increasingly inventive, making use of mōrās and motivic devices. Depending on the creativity and skill of the musicians, the original design idea, seven, may become all but undistinguishable. What follows is a simple koraippu progression using several small mōrās. In these examples the initial eight-pulse *tām* is omitted, though it is included in the notated examples. We will use the following seven-note phrases:

a. ta_2 din_2 ta din_2
b. ta ka din_2 ta din_2
c. ta_2 din_2 gi ṇa tom

STAGE I, PATTERN 2 **(10-118N)**

a b a c
a c c c

Note that by introducing *c* at the end of the first set of four phrases, then stating it three times at the end of the second set of four, we have imitated, on a small scale, the usual pattern of setting up a mōrā by introducing its thematic material into the sarvalaghu that in turn sets it up, as shown below:

ta_2 din_2 ta din_2 ta ka din_2 ta din_2 ta_2 din_2 ta din_2 **ta_2 din_2 gi ṇa tom**
ta_2 din_2 ta din_2 **(ta_2 din_2 gi ṇa tom) (ta_2 din_2 gi ṇa tom) (ta_2 din_2 gi ṇa tom)**

STAGE I, PATTERN 3 **(10-119N)**

This is the first variation on the idea introduced as pattern 2. It is arrived at by altering "c," as follows:

c^5 = ta din gi ṇa tom
c^7 = ta_2 din_2 gi ṇa tom
c^9 = ta_2 din_2 gi_2 $ṇa_2$ tom, so
a b a c^7
a c^5 c^7 c^9

ta_2 din_2 ta din_2 ta ka din_2 ta din_2 ta_2 din_2 ta din_2 **ta_2 din_2 gi ṇa tom**
ta_2 din_2 ta din_2 **(ta din gi ṇa tom) (ta_2 din_2 gi ṇa tom) (ta_2 din_2 gi_2 $ṇa_2$ tom)**

Here c^7 is the original seven-note phrase, so c^5 is arrived at by removing two pulses from the original (one each after *ta* and *din*), and c^9 is arrived at by adding two pulses to the original (one each after *gi* and *ṇa*). The statements in the resulting mōrā still add up to twenty-one pulses, but instead of a sama yati progression, (7) (7) (7), pattern three is an expansion, or srotovaha yati, (5) (7) (9).

STAGE I, PATTERN 4 **(10-120N)**

Simply reverse the order of the mōrā statements in the previous example:

a b a c^7
a c^9 c^7 c^5

Now the mōrā is gopucca yati:

> ta_2 din_2 ta din_2 ta ka din_2 ta din_2 ta_2 din_2 ta din_2 **ta_2 din_2 gi ṇa tom**
> ta_2 din_2 ta din_2 **(ta_2 din_2 gi_2 $ṇa_2$ tom) (ta_2 din_2 gi ṇa tom) (ta din gi ṇa tom)**

We can generate a set of variations on these first four patterns by switching pulse groupings in the second half of each pattern. Leave the first set of four sevens in its original four-per-beat pulse grouping, but change to three pulses per beat for the second half of each group. This leaves space for only three groups of seven each time in the second half. If we just drop the initial *a* in each of the first four patterns, the remaining twenty-one pulses fit perfectly.

STAGE I, PATTERN 5 **(10-121N)**
ta ka di mi ta ki ṭa **ta** ka di mi ta ki ṭa **ta** ka di mi ta ki ṭa **ta** ka di mi ta ki ṭa = seven beats at four pulses per beat
ta ka di mi ta ki ṭa **ta** ka di mi ta ki ṭa **ta** ka di mi ta ki ṭa = seven beats at three pulses per beat

STAGE I, PATTERN 6 **(10-122N)**
ta_2 din_2 ta din_2 ta ka din_2 ta din_2 ta_2 din_2 ta din_2 **ta_2 din_2 gi ṇa tom** = seven beats at four pulses per beat
(ta_2 din_2 gi ṇa tom) (ta_2 din_2 gi ṇa tom) (ta_2 din_2 gi ṇa tom) = seven beats at three pulses per beat

STAGE I, PATTERN 7 **(10-123N)**
ta_2 din_2 ta din_2 ta ka din_2 ta din_2 ta_2 din_2 ta din_2 **ta_2 din_2 gi ṇa tom** = seven beats at four pulses per beat
(ta din gi ṇa tom) (ta_2 din_2 gi ṇa tom) (ta_2 din_2 gi_2 $ṇa_2$ tom) = {seven beats at three pulses per beat

STAGE I, PATTERN 8 **(10-124N)**
ta_2 din_2 ta din_2 ta ka din_2 ta din_2 ta_2 din_2 ta din_2 **ta_2 din_2 gi ṇa tom** = seven beats at four pulses per beat
(ta_2 din_2 gi_2 $ṇa_2$ tom) (ta_2 din_2 gi ṇa tom) (ta din gi ṇa tom) = seven beats at three pulses per beat

Another set of variations becomes possible by substituting the double-time figure *ta_2 kṭ tk tr kṭ tom* for *ta_2 din_2 gi ṇa tom* as *c* in pattern 2 and those that follow.

> *Practice Tip:* In this new phrase, *kṭ tk tr kṭ tom* is short for *ki ṭa ta ka ta ri ki ṭa tom_2*. This phrase can be isolated and practiced in khaṇḍa jāti ēka tāḷa in place of *ta ka ta ki ṭa* until it becomes comfortable. Use the same principle that organized the original seven exercises in tiśra jāti ēka tāḷa (see chapter 1).

STAGE I, PATTERN 9 **(10-125N)**

ta$_2$ din$_2$ ta din$_2$ ta ka din$_2$ ta din$_2$ ta$_2$ din$_2$ ta din$_2$ **ta$_2$ kṭ tk tr kṭ tom**

ta$_2$ din$_2$ ta din$_2$ **(ta$_2$ kṭ tk tr kṭ tom) (ta$_2$ kṭ tk tr kṭ tom) (ta$_2$ kṭ tk tr kṭ tom)**

Use these variations on c, based on the new double time figure, to generate the rest of the mōrās:

c^5 = kṭ tk tr kṭ tom

c^7 = ta$_2$ kṭ tk tr kṭ tom

c^9 = ta$_2$ di$_2$ kṭ tk tr kṭ tom

STAGE I, PATTERN 10 **(10-126N)**

ta$_2$ din$_2$ ta din$_2$ ta ka din$_2$ ta din$_2$ ta$_2$ din$_2$ ta din$_2$ **ta$_2$ kṭ tk tr kṭ tom**

ta$_2$ din$_2$ ta din$_2$ **(kṭ tk tr kṭ tom) (ta$_2$ kṭ tk tr kṭ tom) (ta$_2$ di$_2$ kṭ tk tr kṭ tom)**

STAGE I, PATTERN 11 **(10-127N)**

ta$_2$ din$_2$ ta din$_2$ ta ka din$_2$ ta din$_2$ ta$_2$ din$_2$ ta din$_2$ **ta$_2$ kṭ tk tr kṭ tom**

ta$_2$ din$_2$ ta din$_2$ **(ta$_2$ di$_2$ kṭ tk tr kṭ tom) (ta$_2$ kṭ tk tr kṭ tom) (kṭ tk tr kṭ tom)**

The same process that generated patterns 5 through 8, namely shifting to tiśra naḍai for the second half, produces the last three patterns.

STAGE I, PATTERN 12 **(10-128N)**

ta$_2$ din$_2$ ta din$_2$ ta ka din$_2$ ta din$_2$ ta$_2$ din$_2$ ta din$_2$ **ta$_2$ kṭ tk tr kṭ tom** = {seven beats at four pulses per beat

(ta$_2$ kṭ tk tr kṭ tom) (ta$_2$ kṭ tk tr kṭ tom) (ta$_2$ kṭ tk tr kṭ tom) = seven beats at three pulses per beat

STAGE I, PATTERN 13 **(10-129N)**

ta$_2$ din$_2$ ta din$_2$ ta ka din$_2$ ta din$_2$ ta$_2$ din$_2$ ta din$_2$ **ta$_2$ kṭ tk tr kṭ tom** = seven beats at four pulses per beat

(kṭ tk tr kṭ tom) (ta$_2$ kṭ tk tr kṭ tom) (ta$_2$ di$_2$ kṭ tk tr kṭ tom) = seven beats at three pulses per beat

STAGE I, PATTERN 14 **(10-130N)**

ta$_2$ din$_2$ ta din$_2$ ta ka din$_2$ ta din$_2$ ta$_2$ din$_2$ ta din$_2$ **ta$_2$ kṭ tk tr kṭ tom** = seven beats at four pulses per beat

(ta$_2$ di$_2$ kṭ tk tr kṭ tom) (ta$_2$ kṭ tk tr kṭ tom) (kṭ tk tr kṭ tom) = seven beats at three pulses per beat

Koraippu Stage II

This reduces everything by half, so that each pattern happens within a single cycle. The *tām* that took up eight pulses, or two beats at the beginning of each two-cycle group, in stage I is now four pulses long, or just one beat. The fourteen patterns used are the same as for stage I, but there is only time for the second half of each. Our formula now is $4*1 + 4*7 = 32$.

Here is stage II, pattern 1. Following this example, all fourteen patterns that made up stage I make up stage II, *but only the second half of each.*

STAGE II, PATTERN 1 **(10-131N)**
tām$_4$ **ta** ka di mi ta ki ṭa **ta** ka di mi ta ki ṭa **ta** ka di mi ta ki ṭa **ta** ka di mi ta ki ṭa

Note: In stage I, patterns 5–8 and 12–14 made use of a shift to three pulses per beat at the halfway point. In stage II there is only time for this three-pulse version, so the sense of changing back and forth from four pulses to three will disappear. **(10-132N–10-144N)**

Koraippu Stage III **(10-145N)**

At this stage there is only a half cycle each time. The new formula is $2*1 + 2*7$, as shown in the example:

tām$_2$ **ta** ka di mi ta ki ṭa **ta** ka di mi ta ki ṭa

Since this stage totals only sixteen pulses, there is very little time to generate designs, so trading will focus on the available variations on the seven-pulse phrases given so far:

ta ka di mi ta ki ṭa
ta$_2$ din$_2$ ta din$_2$
ta ka din$_2$ ta din$_2$
ta$_2$ din$_2$ gi ṇa tom
ta$_2$ kṭ tk tr kṭ tom

These phrases should be arranged in pairs. The notated example gives four possibilities; while there are countless others, this sequence will be sufficient for now. The two-pulse *tām* is included in the following patterns.

tām$_2$ ta ka di mi ta ki ṭa **ta** ka di mi ta ki ṭa
tām$_2$ ta$_2$ din$_2$ ta din$_2$ **ta$_2$** din$_2$ gi ṇa tom
tām$_2$ ta ka din$_2$ ta din$_2$ **ta$_2$** din$_2$ gi ṇa tom
tām$_2$ ta$_2$ din$_2$ ta din$_2$ **ta$_2$** kṭ tk tr kṭ tom

Koraippu Stage IV **(10-146N)**

The final stage is only eight pulses, one quarter-cycle long (1 + 7). At this stage, drop out the initial *tām* and leave a one-pulse rest.

Here is one full cycle using the phrase *ta$_2$ din$_2$ gi ṇa tom*:

• ta$_2$ din$_2$ gi ṇa tom • ta$_2$ din$_2$ gi ṇa tom • ta$_2$ din$_2$ gi ṇa tom • ta$_2$ din$_2$ gi ṇa tom

Unison Transition Figure **(10-147N)**

At this point the trading is finished, and only the ending section of the tani remains. Here is a graceful transition to the ending section. It uses the phrase *ta_2 din_2 gi ṇa tom* and removes one pulse from the phrase at each stage. Perform each phrase four times.

ta_2 din_2 gi ṇa tom 7 * 4 = 28
ta din_2 gi ṇa tom 6 * 4 = 24
ta din gi ṇa tom 5 * 4 = 20
din gi ṇa tom 4 * 4 = 16
gi ṇa tom 3 * 4 = 12
ṇa tom 2 * 4 = 8
tom 1 * 4 = 4

So far the pulse total is 112, or three and a half cycles. Here we will add a small mōrā to finish the cycle. Use the fifteen-pulse third mōrā from tiśra jāti ēka tāḷa mōrā series 2, *(ta) [$tām_6$] (ta) [$tām_6$] (ta).*

This mōrā, with its long, sparsely articulated gaps, will provide an effective contrast for the densely articulated transition figure. But it is one pulse short of filling up the half cycle. The simple addition of one more *tom* to the transition section will create an effective connection, as follows:

ta_2 din_2 gi ṇa tom = 28
ta din_2 gi ṇa tom = 24
ta din gi ṇa tom = 20
din gi ṇa tom = 16
gi ṇa tom = 12
ṇa tom = 8
tom*5 (ta) [$tām_6$] (ta) [$tām_6$] (ta) = 128 total pulses, four cycles

The koraippu is now finished. Only the ending section remains. Go directly from the last statement of the mōrā to the *preparation,* the first part of the ending section.

11 · ENDING SECTION

Preparation

As the previous section pointed out, songs in Karnatak music are open-ended in structure. The tani is not bound by anything more than the tāḷa; it is therefore necessary for the drummer or drummers to signal the ensemble that the tani is nearing its end. There are three parts to the ending section, all performed in unison: the preparation; the big (*periya*) mōrā; and a final kōrvai. The first of these, preparation, is characterized by patterns called *paran,* which are more densely articulated than typical sarvalaghu patterns but stay closer to the tāḷa structure than do typical kaṇakku figures. The length and intricacy of this section are discretionary, depending on time, energy, and creativity. The two-stage preparation section that follows is quite brief and relatively simple, but its structure is clear and appropriate to the ending of a tani āvartanam.

The patterns in stage I comprise groups of eight notes, ending with a typical ādi tāḷa mōrā. They are intended to be relatively easy to perform, in contrast to the high degree of rhythmic tension generated by the preceding koraippu. **(11-148N)**

STAGE I PATTERNS

a. tām$_3$ di ta ka jo ṇu

b. tām tām tām di ta ka jo ṇu

STAGE I SEQUENCE

{a*3 b} * 2

{a b} * 4

b*2 + (ta ka jo ṇu) [tām$_2$] (ta ka jo ṇu) [tām$_2$] (ta ka jo ṇu)

The patterns in stage II are slightly more complex but still very close to the tāḷa structure. Four groups of six-note phrases, twenty-four pulses, are followed by two groups of four-note phrases to fill out the cycle. This 24 + 8 sequence is performed twice, after which it is reduced by half. Two groups of six-note phrases are followed by a four-note phrase to make sixteen pulses, or a half cycle. Four sets of this 12 + 4 sequence finish the preparation section.

STAGE II PATTERNS

a. tām$_3$ ta ki ṭa

b. dīm$_3$ ta ki ṭa

c. ta ka di na

d. tom_2 ta_2

STAGE II SEQUENCE

{a*4 c d} {a b a b c d} together done twice

{a a d} {a b c} together done twice, then go directly to periya mōrā

Periya Mōrā

Only two components are actually required for a mrdangam solo to qualify as a tani āvartanam: the periya mōrā and the final kōrvai. The preceding section, the preparation, may be quite brief; it may even be omitted. But the periya mōrā and the final kōrvai are unmistakable signals that the tani is coming to an end and the other musicians must return to the song.

In order to signal the other musicians that the end of the tani is approaching, the periya mōrā must be clearly identifiable as the next-to-last item in the tani. This is accomplished through the use of two devices: its form, and the repeated use of the phrase *ta* $\textit{lān}_2$ *gu* $\textit{tom}_2$ $\textit{ta}_2$ *ta* $\textit{lān}_2$ *gu* $\textit{tom}_4$. While there are many periya mōrās, most contain this distinguishing phrase in order to help identify their function.

The following periya mōrā for ādi tāḷa can be used as a paradigm. Here are the phrases, in unit time. They will be performed in double speed but should first be learned and practiced at half speed:

a. di_4 $tān_2$ giḍu diku taka tari giḍu

b. ta_2 di_2 $tān_2$ giḍu diku taka tari giḍu

c. ta $lān_2$ gu

d. tom_2 ta_2

e. tom_4

This is the sequence of the phrases that make up this periya mōrā:

abacdce * 2

abace

bce

a

(cd)[e]

Here it is, fully written out: **(11-149N)**

di_4 $tān_2$ giḍu diku taka tari giḍu ta_2 di_2 $tān_2$ giḍu diku taka tari giḍu

di_4 $tān_2$ giḍu diku taka tari giḍu **ta $\mathbf{lān_2}$ gu $\mathbf{tom_2}$ $\mathbf{ta_2}$ ta $\mathbf{lān_2}$ gu $\mathbf{tom_4}$**

di_4 $tān_2$ giḍu diku taka tari giḍu ta_2 di_2 $tān_2$ giḍu diku taka tari giḍu

di_4 $tān_2$ giḍu diku taka tari giḍu **ta $\mathbf{lān_2}$ gu $\mathbf{tom_2}$ $\mathbf{ta_2}$ ta $\mathbf{lān_2}$ gu $\mathbf{tom_4}$**

di_4 $tān_2$ giḍu diku taka tari giḍu ta_2 di_2 $tān_2$ giḍu diku taka tari giḍu

di$_4$ tān$_2$ giḍu diku taka tari giḍu **ta lān$_2$ gu tom$_4$**
ta$_2$ di$_2$ tān$_2$ giḍu diku taka tari giḍu **ta lān$_2$ gu tom$_4$**
di$_4$ tān$_2$ giḍu diku taka tari giḍu
(ta lān$_2$ gu tom$_2$ ta$_2$) [tom$_4$]
(ta lān$_2$ gu tom$_2$ ta$_2$) [tom$_4$]
(ta lān$_2$ gu tom$_2$ ta$_2$)

At the notated speed this takes eight cycles of the tāḷa. At its intended performance speed, it takes four cycles. While this duration is not a requirement of the form, it is most often the case. The periya mōrā is performed only once and flows directly into the final kōrvai.

Final Kōrvai

There is no hard and fast rule governing the choice of final kōrvai in a tani āvartanam. It is usually, though not always, chosen to fit easily into the given tāḷa. In other words, a single performance of this kōrvai usually fits neatly into one or two cycles. Because its purpose is to provide a smooth transition back into the song, it is always done three times so the musicians can synchronize their return.

A variety of aesthetic considerations may affect the choice of final kōrvai. For our purposes, we can use it to introduce an internal pulse, or naḍai, that has not been used elsewhere in the tani. This kōrvai is set in *khaṇḍa naḍai*, or five pulses per beat. It also makes use of syllables that are unlike any we have used so far, such as *jem*. It is an old kōrvai, perhaps from the tavil tradition, and comprises eighty total pulses: **(11-150N)**

ta$_2$ ta jem$_2$ jem$_2$ ta ri ta gu gu na ku ku ta$_2$ di$_3$ = 20 pulses
gu gu na na ku din$_2$ din$_2$ gu di ku na ku ku ta$_2$ di$_3$ = 20 pulses
ta$_2$ ta jem$_2$ jem$_2$ ta ri$_2$ = 10 pulses
• • ta jem$_2$ jem$_2$ ta ri$_2$ = 10 pulses
ta$_2$ ta jem$_2$ = 5 pulses
(ta di ki ṭa tom) (ta di ki ṭa tom) (ta di ki ṭa tom) = 15 pulses

Note that the phrases fall neatly into groups of five pulses. In contrast with the material done previously in tiśra naḍai, in which phrases grouped in fours and sevens were performed at the three-pulse-per-beat rate, the phrases in this kōrvai are quite easy to follow, making it an effective ending.

CONCLUSION

12 · PUTTING IT ALL TOGETHER

For most people working with this book, the most rewarding thing to do with all of the material will be to perform it. You can design any number of performance pieces using the sarvalaghus, mōrās, kōrvais, koraippu, and ending section to suit your own situation. The accompanying video includes three such pieces, for one, two, and four players, respectively. Each of these uses some material from the lessons and leaves out other material. Deciding what to include or leave out depends on how long a piece you want, how many people are involved, what their skill levels are, and what interests you the most. There are very few hard and fast rules about doing this within the Karnatak definition of the tani āvartanam; the following suggestions will help keep your piece on track and within the idiom.

First, the only items a tani *must* include are the periya mōrā and final kōrvai. There are times when a solo must be extremely brief; in these cases the last two parts of the ending section identify the function of the solo as a tani, rather than just an extended mōrā. The usual practice is to perform these two parts in unison, but this is not a requirement. You can experiment with breaking up the sections among your performers as you wish.

Next, a koraippu is seldom, if ever, performed by a solo artist. It requires at least two players. The most important performers in the koraippu are the person who begins each section and the person who ends it. I try to put my most reliable players at the ends of the line. Most mistakes in a solkaṭṭu piece, and those most difficult to recover from, will happen in the koraippu. An unflappable person at the head of the line can keep an otherwise wonderful piece from falling apart in this tricky section.

Finally, the order of the sarvalaghu should be maintained in roughly the order presented in the ādi tāḷa lessons. If you perform them in another order an informed listener will probably not accept your piece as a proper tani. You may, however, leave out whole sections as you wish.

I arranged three pieces for the video, each of which demonstrates ways to tailor the material to a given situation. What follows is an explanation of each piece—its structure as well as observations about the actual performance.

Tani for One Player

I performed the solo piece without any written plan, though I arranged it so that it would take about ten minutes and rehearsed it carefully. Here is its structure.

TANI FOR ONE PLAYER

ādi tāḷa, oru kaḷai, MM±60

I. ādi tāḷa sarvalaghu and mōrās
   a. ādi mōrās 1, 2, and 3
   b. compound mōrā 4
   c. arudi

II. Palani Subramania Pillai composition in three speeds, followed by arudi

III. kōrvai 1 with setup, twice
   a. original speed
   b. tiśra naḍai, six pulses per beat

IV. tiśra kōrvai with setup
   a. original
   b. variation 2
   c. variation 3
   d. arudi

V. ending section
   a. preparation
   b. periya mōrā
   c. final kōrvai

Notice that I performed kōrvai 1 twice, or "once and once," as suggested at the end of chapter 8. By performing the kōrvai first in caturaśra naḍai and then in tiśra naḍai I made a smooth transition into the latter pulse rate, setting up the tiśra kōrvai. Because this was a solo piece, I omitted the miśra koraippu entirely, going directly from the tiśra kōrvai to the ending section. As you will see in the other pieces, whole sections may be altered or left out according to the situation.

Tani for Two Players

I designed this piece to be about twelve minutes long. I made the following outline and sent it to my student Geoff Brown (GB in the outline), along with notation for each section. We rehearsed it once the day before the recording. The version on the video is the third take from the recording session. The only notation we used was the outline:

TANI FOR TWO PLAYERS

ādi tāḷa, oru kaḷai, MM±60

I. ādi tāḷa sarvalaghu and mōrās
   a. ādi mōrā 1: DN

b. ādi mōrā 2: GB from stage III
c. compound mōrā 5, from stage IV: DN, GB, both
d. arudi: both

II. ādi tāḷa kōrvai
a. kōrvai 1, variation 5: GB
b. kōrvai 1, variation 5, tiśra naḍai, three pulses per beat: DN
c. arudi: both

III. miśra koraippu
a. stage 1, patterns 1, 3, 9, 11, 13: DN; patterns 2, 4, 10, 12, 14: GB
b. stage 2, same sequences, second half only
c. stage 3, two lines each
d. stage 4, twice
e. unison ending section: both

IV. ending, both
a. preparation, notation 11-1
b. periya mōrā, notation 11-2
c. final kōrvai, 11-3

After alternating the first two ādi tāḷa mōrās we go directly to compound mōrā 5, starting from stage IV. This compound mōrā begins with ādi mōrā 3, which lends a slight deception to this section of the tani. The ear may hear ādi mōrā 3 as a logical continuation of the first two, but it begins on the "wrong" beat seven (where the compound mōrās begin) instead of three (where the simple mōrās begin).

The Palani Subramania Pillai composition is omitted from this tani in the interest of keeping it short and interesting. The next section is the ādi tāḷa kōrvai, which, as in the solo piece, is performed twice. This time, however, we use the filled-out version, even in the setup. The tiśra naḍai version is done at three pulses per beat, because the double-speed phrases would be quite difficult at six pulses per beat. This, like the previous version, is suggested at the end of chapter 8 as a transition to the tiśra naḍai section of the tani. In this case, however, its purpose is not to set up such a transition but to stand on its own.

The next section is the miśra koraippu. Here we omit patterns 5 through 8 from the first two stages; remember that nearly any segment may be omitted in the interest of time.

Notice that there is a mistake toward the end of the second stage. *Mistakes are going to happen!* I have witnessed and performed scores of koraippus in the last thirty years. It is safe to say that the majority of them have included mistakes. While we try our best to avoid them, any Karnatak musician will tell you that mistakes are part of the music. One can only try to recover as quickly as possible and avoid interrupting the momentum any more than necessary. In this case I have myself to blame for the mistake and Geoff Brown to thank for a smooth recovery. Displeased as I was with myself, I was extremely proud of my student. While we could have held out for a "perfect" take, I decided that this mistake and recovery would make a fine teaching example, and we left it alone. The great pianist, composer, and improviser Thelonious Monk is reported, perhaps apocryphally, to have said of jazz, "There are two kinds of mistakes—the regular kind, and the kind that don't sound so good." The same goes for Karnatak music.

Tani for Four Players

At twenty-four minutes this is the longest of the three pieces, and the most similar to the performance piece that comes at the end of spring term each year. I did not have ready access to members of a solkaṭṭu class, because I was on sabbatical at the time, so I needed to find students who were willing and able to come to Wesleyan in the summer. Ruby Ross had taken my solkaṭṭu course, while Aaron Paige (class of 2004) and Dennis Chan (class of 2006) learned mrdangam from me as Wesleyan students. Geoff Brown, a talented Hartford-area percussionist, has been learning solkaṭṭu and kanjira for three years as my private student. I sent them the following outline and supporting notation, and they came together on the day of the recording. After a brief rehearsal, they performed the entire piece twice, with very few interruptions. While we did not get a perfectly clean single version of this long piece, we were able to put the best of the two versions together with a single edit, at the beginning of the koraippu. The fact that these musicians had never performed together, and in some cases had not even met before, makes their work together all the more remarkable. I am deeply grateful to all of them.

TANI FOR FOUR PLAYERS

ādi tāḷa, oru kaḷai, MM±60

I. ādi tāḷa mōrās
   a. ādi mōrā 1: all
   b. ādi mōrā 2: RR, AP
   c. ādi mōrā 3: GB, DC
   d. compound mōrā 4: RR, AP
   e. compound mōrā 5: GB, DC
   f. arudi: all

II. Palani Subramania Pillai composition
   a. slow caturaśra: all
   b. tiśra naḍai: RR, AP
   c. fast caturaśra: GB, DC
   d. arudi: all

III. ādi tāḷa kōrvai
   a. kōrvai 1: RR
   b. kōrvai 1 variation 3: AP
   c. kōrvai 1 variation 5: GB
   d. kōrvai 1 variation 8: DC
   e. arudi: all

IV. tiśra kōrvai
   a. tiśra kōrvai setup: all
   b. tiśra kōrvai original: RR, AP
   c. tiśra kōrvai variation 2: GB, DC
   d. tiśra kōrvai variation 3: all
   e. arudi: all

V. miśra koraippu
   a. stage 1.
      i. patterns 1–4, 5–8, 9–12: RR, AP, GB, DC
      ii. pattern 13: RR, AP
      iii. pattern 14: GB, DC
   b. stage 2: same sequences, second half only
   c. stage 3: one line each
   d. stage 4: twice
   e. unison ending section: all

VI. ending section: all
   a. preparation
   b. periya mōrā
   c. final kōrvai

This is the most complete tani in terms of the contents of the text. All six sets of lessons are represented and for the most part conform to the notated examples. One exception is the mōrā in Dennis Chan's version of kōrvai 1, in which the statements (c^2 c^4 c^6) reverse the order in the notation (c^6 c^4 c^2). At the time I thought he was improvising, which was fine with me, because either order will come out right. It turned out that there was a mistake in the notation, which I have since corrected. The only significant "mistake" in this tani comes, as before, in the koraippu, midway through the third stage. Ruby Ross attempts to correct herself and is not able to do so. Aaron Paige, next in line, stumbles as a result. Once again the estimable Geoff Brown comes to the rescue, recovering from the mistake. Again, this is a misstep with real value. A mistake such as Ruby's can generate a cascade effect, resulting in a complete breakdown. A successful recovery, however, can infuse a performance with new energy and humor, a vibrant sense that all's well that ends well. Such was the case with this performance, which left the performers exhilarated and the teacher deeply gratified.

. . .

The three pieces presented here are by no means meant to be exhaustive. You may copy them if you wish; it might be quite useful to do so. But the real purpose of these performances is to spark your imagination. Perhaps your class has ten or twenty people. Some of them will be much stronger than others. You can arrange this material in such a way that the strongest people have the most difficult parts and take solos, while others can work on less challenging material without having to go it alone. It is possible to put pieces together that engage and challenge people of widely divergent abilities. One of the beauties of solkaṭṭu is this ability to give everybody something that will challenge him or her, no matter what the skill level.

NOTATION

01-002N

tiśra jāti ēka tāḷa — trikāla without pulses

<table>
<tr><td colspan="4">| clap</td><td colspan="4">• pinky</td><td colspan="4">• ring</td></tr>
<tr><td colspan="12">first speed</td></tr>
<tr><td colspan="4">|ta</td><td colspan="4">|ki</td><td colspan="4">|ṭa</td></tr>
<tr><td colspan="4">|ta</td><td colspan="4">|ki</td><td colspan="4">|ṭa</td></tr>
<tr><td colspan="4">|ta</td><td colspan="4">|ki</td><td colspan="4">|ṭa</td></tr>
<tr><td colspan="4">|ta</td><td colspan="4">|ki</td><td colspan="4">|ṭa</td></tr>
<tr><td colspan="12">second speed</td></tr>
<tr><td colspan="2">|ta</td><td colspan="2">ki</td><td colspan="2">|ṭa</td><td colspan="2">ta</td><td colspan="2">|ki</td><td colspan="2">ṭa</td></tr>
<tr><td colspan="2">|ta</td><td colspan="2">ki</td><td colspan="2">|ṭa</td><td colspan="2">ta</td><td colspan="2">|ki</td><td colspan="2">ṭa</td></tr>
<tr><td colspan="2">|ta</td><td colspan="2">ki</td><td colspan="2">|ṭa</td><td colspan="2">ta</td><td colspan="2">|ki</td><td colspan="2">ṭa</td></tr>
<tr><td colspan="2">|ta</td><td colspan="2">ki</td><td colspan="2">|ṭa</td><td colspan="2">ta</td><td colspan="2">|ki</td><td colspan="2">ṭa</td></tr>
<tr><td colspan="12">third speed</td></tr>
<tr><td>|ta</td><td>ki</td><td>ṭa</td><td>ta</td><td>|ki</td><td>ṭa</td><td>ta</td><td>ki</td><td>|ṭa</td><td>ta</td><td>ki</td><td>ṭa</td></tr>
<tr><td>|ta</td><td>ki</td><td>ṭa</td><td>ta</td><td>|ki</td><td>ṭa</td><td>ta</td><td>ki</td><td>|ṭa</td><td>ta</td><td>ki</td><td>ṭa</td></tr>
<tr><td>|ta</td><td>ki</td><td>ṭa</td><td>ta</td><td>|ki</td><td>ṭa</td><td>ta</td><td>ki</td><td>|ṭa</td><td>ta</td><td>ki</td><td>ṭa</td></tr>
<tr><td>|ta</td><td>ki</td><td>ṭa</td><td>ta</td><td>|ki</td><td>ṭa</td><td>ta</td><td>ki</td><td>|ṭa</td><td>ta</td><td>ki</td><td>ṭa</td></tr>
</table>

tiśra jāti ēka tāḷa

01-003N

exercise 1: trikāla

|				•				•			

first speed

|**ta**	-	-	-	|ki	-	-	-	|ṭa	-	-	-
|**ta**	-	-	-	|ki	-	-	-	|ṭa	-	-	-
|**ta**	-	-	-	|ki	-	-	-	|ṭa	-	-	-
|**ta**	-	-	-	|ki	-	-	-	|ṭa	-	-	-

second speed

|**ta**	-	ki	-	|ṭa	-	**ta**	-	|ki	-	ṭa	-
|**ta**	-	ki	-	|ṭa	-	**ta**	-	|ki	-	ṭa	-
|**ta**	-	ki	-	|ṭa	-	**ta**	-	|ki	-	ṭa	-
|**ta**	-	ki	-	|ṭa	-	**ta**	-	|ki	-	ṭa	-

third speed

|**ta**	ki	ṭa	**ta**	|ki	ṭa	**ta**	ki	|ṭa	**ta**	ki	ṭa
|**ta**	ki	ṭa	**ta**	|ki	ṭa	**ta**	ki	|ṭa	**ta**	ki	ṭa
|**ta**	ki	ṭa	**ta**	|ki	ṭa	**ta**	ki	|ṭa	**ta**	ki	ṭa
|**ta**	ki	ṭa	**ta**	|ki	ṭa	**ta**	ki	|ṭa	**ta**	ki	ṭa

01-004N

tiśra jāti ēka tāḷa

exercise 2: slow fast fast

I				•				•			
|**ta**	-	ki	-	|ṭa	-	**ta**	ki	|ṭa	**ta**	ki	ṭa
|**ta**	-	ki	-	|ṭa	-	**ta**	ki	|ṭa	**ta**	ki	ṭa
|**ta**	-	ki	-	|ṭa	-	**ta**	ki	|ṭa	**ta**	ki	ṭa
|**ta**	-	ki	-	|ṭa	-	**ta**	ki	|ṭa	**ta**	ki	ṭa

01-005N

tiśra jāti ēka tāḷa

exercise 3: fast fast slow

I				•				•			
|**ta**	ki	ṭa	**ta**	|ki	ṭa	**ta**	-	|ki	-	ṭa	-
|**ta**	ki	ṭa	**ta**	|ki	ṭa	**ta**	-	|ki	-	ṭa	-
|**ta**	ki	ṭa	**ta**	|ki	ṭa	**ta**	-	|ki	-	ṭa	-
|**ta**	ki	ṭa	**ta**	|ki	ṭa	**ta**	-	|ki	-	ṭa	-

01-006N
exercise 4: fast slow fast

tiśra jāti ēka tāḷa

|				•				•			
|**ta**	ki	ṭa	**ta**	|-	ki	-	ṭa	|-	**ta**	ki	ṭa
|**ta**	ki	ṭa	**ta**	|-	ki	-	ṭa	|-	**ta**	ki	ṭa
|**ta**	ki	ṭa	**ta**	|-	ki	-	ṭa	|-	**ta**	ki	ṭa
|**ta**	ki	ṭa	**ta**	|-	ki	-	ṭa	|-	**ta**	ki	ṭa

01-007N
exercise 5: three plus one

tiśra jāti ēka tāḷa

|				•				•			
|**ta**	-	-	ki	|-	-	ṭa	-	|-	**ta**	ki	ṭa
|**ta**	-	-	ki	|-	-	ṭa	-	|-	**ta**	ki	ṭa
|**ta**	-	-	ki	|-	-	ṭa	-	|-	**ta**	ki	ṭa
|**ta**	-	-	ki	|-	-	ṭa	-	|-	**ta**	ki	ṭa

01-008N

exercise 6: one plus three

tiśra jāti ēka tāḷa

I				•				•			
ta	ki	ṭa	**ta**	-	-	ki	-	-	ṭa	-	-
ta	ki	ṭa	**ta**	-	-	ki	-	-	ṭa	-	-
ta	ki	ṭa	**ta**	-	-	ki	-	-	ṭa	-	-
ta	ki	ṭa	**ta**	-	-	ki	-	-	ṭa	-	-

01-012N

exercise 7: four speeds

tiśra jāti ēka tāḷa

I				•				•			
-	-	-	-	-	-	**ta**	-	-	-	ki	-
-	-	ṭa	-	-	-	**ta**	-	-	ki	-	-
ṭa	-	-	**ta**	-	ki	-	ṭa	-	**ta**	ki	ṭa

02-017N

tiśra jāti ēka tāḷa — second series pattern 1

I				•				•			
Stage I											
|**ta**	-	ka	ta	|ka	-	**ta**	-	|ka	ta	ka	-
|**ta**	-	ka	ta	|ka	-	**ta**	-	|ka	ta	ka	-
|**ta**	-	ka	ta	|ka	-	**ta**	-	|ka	ta	ka	-
|**ta**	-	ka	ta	|ka	-	**ta**	ka	|-	ta	-	ka
|**ta**	-	ka	ta	|ka	-	**ta**	-	|ka	ta	ka	-
|**ta**	-	ka	ta	|ka	-	**ta**	-	|ka	ta	ka	-
|**ta**	-	ka	ta	|ka	-	**ta**	-	|ka	ta	ka	-
|**ta**	-	ka	ta	|ka	-	**ta**	ka	|-	ta	-	ka
Stage II											
|**ta**	-	ka	ta	|ka	-	**ta**	-	|ka	ta	ka	-
|**ta**	-	ka	ta	|ka	-	**ta**	ka	|-	ta	-	ka
|**ta**	-	ka	ta	|ka	-	**ta**	-	|ka	ta	ka	-
|**ta**	-	ka	ta	|ka	-	**ta**	ka	|-	ta	-	ka

Stage III

<table>
<tr><td>|ta</td><td>-</td><td>ka</td><td>ta</td><td>|ka</td><td>-</td><td>ta</td><td>ka</td><td>|-</td><td>ta</td><td>-</td><td>ka</td></tr>
<tr><td>|ta</td><td>-</td><td>ka</td><td>ta</td><td>|ka</td><td>-</td><td>ta</td><td>ka</td><td>|-</td><td>ta</td><td>-</td><td>ka</td></tr>
<tr><td>|ta</td><td>-</td><td>ka</td><td>ta</td><td>|ka</td><td>-</td><td>ta</td><td>ka</td><td>|-</td><td>ta</td><td>-</td><td>ka</td></tr>
<tr><td>|ta</td><td>-</td><td>ka</td><td>ta</td><td>|ka</td><td>-</td><td>ta</td><td>ka</td><td>|-</td><td>ta</td><td>-</td><td>ka</td></tr>
</table>

Stage IV

<table>
<tr><td>|ta</td><td>ka</td><td>-</td><td>ta</td><td>|-</td><td>ka</td><td>ta</td><td>ka</td><td>|-</td><td>ta</td><td>-</td><td>ka</td></tr>
<tr><td>|ta</td><td>ka</td><td>-</td><td>ta</td><td>|-</td><td>ka</td><td>ta</td><td>ka</td><td>|-</td><td>ta</td><td>-</td><td>ka</td></tr>
</table>

Stage V

<table>
<tr><td>|ta</td><td>ka</td><td>-</td><td>ta</td><td>|ka</td><td>-</td><td>ta</td><td>ka</td><td>|-</td><td>ta</td><td>ka</td><td>-</td></tr>
</table>

02-027N

tiśra jāti ēka tāḷa — second series pattern 2

I				•				•			
Stage I											
|**din**	-	ta	ta	|din	-	**din**	-	|ta	ta	din	-
|**din**	-	ta	ta	|din	-	**din**	-	|ta	ta	din	-
|**din**	-	ta	ta	|din	-	**din**	-	|ta	ta	din	-
|**din**	-	ta	ta	|din	-	**ta**	din	|-	din	-	ta
|**din**	-	ta	ta	|din	-	**din**	-	|ta	ta	din	-
|**din**	-	ta	ta	|din	-	**din**	-	|ta	ta	din	-
|**din**	-	ta	ta	|din	-	**din**	-	|ta	ta	din	-
|**din**	-	ta	ta	|din	-	**ta**	din	|-	din	-	ta
Stage II											
|**din**	-	ta	ta	|din	-	**din**	-	|ta	ta	din	-
|**din**	-	ta	ta	|din	-	**ta**	din	|-	din	-	ta
|**din**	-	ta	ta	|din	-	**din**	-	|ta	ta	din	-
|**din**	-	ta	ta	|din	-	**ta**	din	|-	din	-	ta

Stage III

|**din** - ta ta |din - **ta** din |- din - ta

|**din** - ta ta |din - **ta** din |- din - ta

|**din** - ta ta |din - **ta** din |- din - ta

|**din** - ta ta |din - **ta** din |- din - ta

Stage IV

|**ta** din - din |- ta **ta** din |- din - ta

|**ta** din - din |- ta **ta** din |- din - ta

Stage V

|**ta** din - **ta** |din - **ta** din |- **ta** din -

|**tām**

03-031N

tiśra jāti ēka tāḷa

mōrā series 1, mōrā 1

|				•				•			
Stage I											
|**din**	-	ta	ta	|din	-	**din**	-	|ta	ta	din	-
|**din**	-	ta	ta	|din	-	**din**	-	|ta	ta	din	-
|**din**	-	ta	ta	|din	-	**din**	-	|ta	ta	din	-
|**din**	-	ta	ta	|din	-	**ta**	din	|-	din	-	ta
|**din**	-	ta	ta	|din	-	**din**	-	|ta	ta	din	-
|**din**	-	ta	ta	|din	-	**din**	-	|ta	ta	din	-
|**din**	-	ta	ta	|din	-	**din**	-	|ta	ta	din	-
|**din**	-	ta	ta	|din	-	**ta**	din	|-	din	-	ta
Stage II											
|**din**	-	ta	ta	|din	-	**din**	-	|ta	ta	din	-
|**din**	-	ta	ta	|din	-	**ta**	din	|-	din	-	ta
|**din**	-	ta	ta	|din	-	**din**	-	|ta	ta	din	-
|**din**	-	ta	ta	|din	-	**ta**	din	|-	din	-	ta

Stage III

|**din** - ta ta |din - **ta** din |- din - ta

|**din** - ta ta |din - **ta** din |- din - ta

|**din** - ta ta |din - **ta** din |- din - ta

|**din** - ta ta |din - **ta** din |- din - ta

Stage IV

|**ta** din - din |- ta **ta** din |- din - ta

|**ta** din - din |- ta **ta** din |- din - ta

Stage V + mōrā 1

|**ta** din - **ta** |din - **ta** din |- **ta** din -

|**tām** - - - |- (ta) [tām -] |(ta) [tām -] (ta)

tiśra jāti ēka tāḷa

03-033N
mōrā series 1, mōrā 2

| • •

Stage III

|**din** - ta ta |din - **ta** din |- din - ta

|**din** - ta ta |din - **ta** din |- din - ta

|**din** - ta ta |din - **ta** din |- din - ta

|**din** - ta ta |din - **ta** din |- din - ta

Stage IV

|**ta** din - din |- ta **ta** din |- din - ta

|**ta** din - din |- ta **ta** din |- din - ta

Stage V+ mōrā 2

|**ta** din - **ta** |din - **ta** din |- tam - -

|- - (din ta) |[tam -] (din ta) |[tam -] (din ta)

03-034N

tiśra jāti ēka tāḷa — mōrā series 1, mōrā 3

<table>
<tr><td>|</td><td></td><td></td><td></td><td>•</td><td></td><td></td><td></td><td>•</td><td></td><td></td><td></td></tr>
<tr><td colspan="12">Stage III</td></tr>
<tr><td>|din</td><td>-</td><td>ta</td><td>ta</td><td>|din</td><td>-</td><td>ta</td><td>din</td><td>|-</td><td>din</td><td>-</td><td>ta</td></tr>
<tr><td>|din</td><td>-</td><td>ta</td><td>ta</td><td>|din</td><td>-</td><td>ta</td><td>din</td><td>|-</td><td>din</td><td>-</td><td>ta</td></tr>
<tr><td>|din</td><td>-</td><td>ta</td><td>ta</td><td>|din</td><td>-</td><td>ta</td><td>din</td><td>|-</td><td>din</td><td>-</td><td>ta</td></tr>
<tr><td>|din</td><td>-</td><td>ta</td><td>ta</td><td>|din</td><td>-</td><td>ta</td><td>din</td><td>|-</td><td>din</td><td>-</td><td>ta</td></tr>
<tr><td colspan="12">Stage IV</td></tr>
<tr><td>|ta</td><td>din</td><td>-</td><td>din</td><td>|-</td><td>ta</td><td>ta</td><td>din</td><td>|-</td><td>din</td><td>-</td><td>ta</td></tr>
<tr><td>|ta</td><td>din</td><td>-</td><td>din</td><td>|-</td><td>ta</td><td>ta</td><td>din</td><td>|-</td><td>din</td><td>-</td><td>ta</td></tr>
<tr><td colspan="12">Stage V+ mōrā 3</td></tr>
<tr><td>|ta</td><td>din</td><td>-</td><td>ta</td><td>|din</td><td>-</td><td>tam</td><td>-</td><td>|-</td><td>-</td><td>-</td><td>(ka</td></tr>
<tr><td>|din</td><td>ta)</td><td>[tam</td><td>-]</td><td>|(ka</td><td>din</td><td>ta)</td><td>[tam</td><td>|-]</td><td>(ka</td><td>din</td><td>ta)</td></tr>
</table>

03-035N

tiśra jāti ēka tāḷa — mōrā series 1, mōrā 4

I				•				•			
Stage III											
|**din**	-	ta	ta	|din	-	**ta**	din	|-	din	-	ta
|**din**	-	ta	ta	|din	-	**ta**	din	|-	din	-	ta
|**din**	-	ta	ta	|din	-	**ta**	din	|-	din	-	ta
|**din**	-	ta	ta	|din	-	**ta**	din	|-	din	-	ta
Stage IV											
|**ta**	din	-	din	|-	ta	**ta**	din	|-	din	-	ta
|**ta**	din	-	din	|-	ta	**ta**	din	|-	din	-	ta
Stage V+ mōrā 4											
|**ta**	din	-	tam	|-	-	-	-	|(ta	ka	din	ta)
|[tam	-]	(ta	ka	|din	ta)	[tam	-]	|(ta	ka	din	ta)

03-036N

tiśra jāti ēka tāḷa

mōrā series 1, mōrā 5

| • •

<table>
<tr><td colspan="12">Stage III</td></tr>
<tr><td>|din</td><td>-</td><td>ta</td><td>ta</td><td>|din</td><td>-</td><td>ta</td><td>din</td><td>|-</td><td>din</td><td>-</td><td>ta</td></tr>
<tr><td>|din</td><td>-</td><td>ta</td><td>ta</td><td>|din</td><td>-</td><td>ta</td><td>din</td><td>|-</td><td>din</td><td>-</td><td>ta</td></tr>
<tr><td>|din</td><td>-</td><td>ta</td><td>ta</td><td>|din</td><td>-</td><td>ta</td><td>din</td><td>|-</td><td>din</td><td>-</td><td>ta</td></tr>
<tr><td>|din</td><td>-</td><td>ta</td><td>ta</td><td>|din</td><td>-</td><td>ta</td><td>din</td><td>|-</td><td>din</td><td>-</td><td>ta</td></tr>
<tr><td colspan="12">Stage IV</td></tr>
<tr><td>|ta</td><td>din</td><td>-</td><td>din</td><td>|-</td><td>ta</td><td>ta</td><td>din</td><td>|-</td><td>din</td><td>-</td><td>ta</td></tr>
<tr><td>|ta</td><td>din</td><td>-</td><td>din</td><td>|-</td><td>ta</td><td>ta</td><td>din</td><td>|-</td><td>din</td><td>-</td><td>ta</td></tr>
<tr><td colspan="12">Stage V+ mōrā 5</td></tr>
<tr><td>|ta</td><td>din</td><td>-</td><td>tam</td><td>|-</td><td>-</td><td>-</td><td>-</td><td>|(ta</td><td>ka</td><td>din</td><td>ta)</td></tr>
<tr><td>|[tam</td><td>-]</td><td>(ka</td><td>din</td><td>|ta)</td><td>[tam</td><td>-]</td><td>(din</td><td>|ta)</td><td>[tam</td><td>-]</td><td>(ta)</td></tr>
</table>

03-037N

tiśra jāti ēka tāḷa

mōrā series 1, mōrā 6

I				•				•			
Stage III											
|**din**	-	ta	ta	|din	-	**ta**	din	|-	din	-	ta
|**din**	-	ta	ta	|din	-	**ta**	din	|-	din	-	ta
|**din**	-	ta	ta	|din	-	**ta**	din	|-	din	-	ta
|**din**	-	ta	ta	|din	-	**ta**	din	|-	din	-	ta
Stage IV											
|**ta**	din	-	din	|-	ta	**ta**	din	|-	din	-	ta
|**ta**	din	-	din	|-	ta	**ta**	din	|-	din	-	ta
Stage V+ mōrā 6											
|**ta**	din	-	tam	|-	-	-	-	|(ta)	[tam	-]	(din
|ta)	[tam	-]	(ka	|din	ta)	[tam	-]	|(ta	ka	din	ta)

04-039N

tiśra jāti ēka tāḷa

mōrā series 2, setup and mōrā 1

|				•				•			
Stage I											
|**din**	-	ta	ta	|din	-	**din**	-	|ta	ta	din	-
|**din**	-	ta	ta	|din	-	**din**	-	|ta	ta	din	-
|**din**	-	ta	ta	|din	-	**din**	-	|ta	ta	din	-
|**din**	-	ta	ta	|din	-	**ta**	din	|-	din	-	ta
|**din**	-	ta	ta	|din	-	**din**	-	|ta	ta	din	-
|**din**	-	ta	ta	|din	-	**din**	-	|ta	ta	din	-
|**din**	-	ta	ta	|din	-	**din**	-	|ta	ta	din	-
|**din**	-	ta	ta	|din	-	**ta**	din	|-	din	-	ta
Stage II											
|**din**	-	ta	ta	|din	-	**din**	-	|ta	ta	din	-
|**din**	-	ta	ta	|din	-	**ta**	din	|-	din	-	ta
|**din**	-	ta	ta	|din	-	**din**	-	|ta	ta	din	-
|**din**	-	ta	ta	|din	-	**ta**	din	|-	din	-	ta

continued

continued

<table>
<tr><td colspan="12">Stage III</td></tr>
<tr><td>|din</td><td>-</td><td>ta</td><td>ta</td><td>|din</td><td>-</td><td>ta</td><td>din</td><td>|-</td><td>din</td><td>-</td><td>ta</td></tr>
<tr><td>|din</td><td>-</td><td>ta</td><td>ta</td><td>|din</td><td>-</td><td>ta</td><td>din</td><td>|-</td><td>din</td><td>-</td><td>ta</td></tr>
<tr><td>|din</td><td>-</td><td>ta</td><td>ta</td><td>|din</td><td>-</td><td>ta</td><td>din</td><td>|-</td><td>din</td><td>-</td><td>ta</td></tr>
<tr><td>|din</td><td>-</td><td>ta</td><td>ta</td><td>|din</td><td>-</td><td>ta</td><td>din</td><td>|-</td><td>din</td><td>-</td><td>ta</td></tr>
<tr><td colspan="12">Stage IV</td></tr>
<tr><td>|ta</td><td>din</td><td>-</td><td>din</td><td>|-</td><td>ta</td><td>ta</td><td>din</td><td>|-</td><td>din</td><td>-</td><td>ta</td></tr>
<tr><td>|ta</td><td>din</td><td>-</td><td>din</td><td>|-</td><td>ta</td><td>ta</td><td>din</td><td>|-</td><td>din</td><td>-</td><td>ta</td></tr>
<tr><td colspan="12">Stage V + mōrā 1</td></tr>
<tr><td>|ta</td><td>-</td><td>-</td><td>ka</td><td>|-</td><td>-</td><td>di</td><td>-</td><td>|-</td><td>mi</td><td>-</td><td>-</td></tr>
<tr><td>|ta</td><td>ka</td><td>ta</td><td>ki</td><td>|ṭa</td><td>(ta)</td><td>[tām</td><td>-]</td><td>|(ta)</td><td>[tām</td><td>-]</td><td>(ta)</td></tr>
</table>

04-040N

tiśra jāti ēka tāḷa — mōrā series 2, mōrā 2

| • •

Stage III

<table>
<tr><td>|din</td><td>-</td><td>ta</td><td>ta</td><td>|din</td><td>-</td><td>ta</td><td>din</td><td>|-</td><td>din</td><td>-</td><td>ta</td></tr>
<tr><td>|din</td><td>-</td><td>ta</td><td>ta</td><td>|din</td><td>-</td><td>ta</td><td>din</td><td>|-</td><td>din</td><td>-</td><td>ta</td></tr>
<tr><td>|din</td><td>-</td><td>ta</td><td>ta</td><td>|din</td><td>-</td><td>ta</td><td>din</td><td>|-</td><td>din</td><td>-</td><td>ta</td></tr>
<tr><td>|din</td><td>-</td><td>ta</td><td>ta</td><td>|din</td><td>-</td><td>ta</td><td>din</td><td>|-</td><td>din</td><td>-</td><td>ta</td></tr>
</table>

Stage IV

<table>
<tr><td>|ta</td><td>din</td><td>-</td><td>din</td><td>|-</td><td>ta</td><td>ta</td><td>din</td><td>|-</td><td>din</td><td>-</td><td>ta</td></tr>
<tr><td>|ta</td><td>din</td><td>-</td><td>din</td><td>|-</td><td>ta</td><td>ta</td><td>din</td><td>|-</td><td>din</td><td>-</td><td>ta</td></tr>
</table>

Stage V+ mōrā 2

<table>
<tr><td>|ta</td><td>-</td><td>ka</td><td>-</td><td>|di</td><td>-</td><td>mi</td><td>-</td><td>|ta</td><td>ka</td><td>ta</td><td>ki</td></tr>
<tr><td>|ṭa</td><td>(ta)</td><td>[tam</td><td>-</td><td>|-</td><td>-]</td><td>(ta)</td><td>[tam</td><td>|-</td><td>-</td><td>-]</td><td>(ta)</td></tr>
</table>

04-041N

tiśra jāti ēka tāḷa

mōrā series 2, mōrā 3

<table>
<tr><td>|</td><td></td><td></td><td></td><td>•</td><td></td><td></td><td></td><td>•</td><td></td><td></td><td></td></tr>
<tr><td colspan="12">Stage III</td></tr>
<tr><td>|din</td><td>-</td><td>ta</td><td>ta</td><td>|din</td><td>-</td><td>ta</td><td>din</td><td>|-</td><td>din</td><td>-</td><td>ta</td></tr>
<tr><td>|din</td><td>-</td><td>ta</td><td>ta</td><td>|din</td><td>-</td><td>ta</td><td>din</td><td>|-</td><td>din</td><td>-</td><td>ta</td></tr>
<tr><td>|din</td><td>-</td><td>ta</td><td>ta</td><td>|din</td><td>-</td><td>ta</td><td>din</td><td>|-</td><td>din</td><td>-</td><td>ta</td></tr>
<tr><td>|din</td><td>-</td><td>ta</td><td>ta</td><td>|din</td><td>-</td><td>ta</td><td>din</td><td>|-</td><td>din</td><td>-</td><td>ta</td></tr>
<tr><td colspan="12">Stage IV</td></tr>
<tr><td>|ta</td><td>din</td><td>-</td><td>din</td><td>|-</td><td>ta</td><td>ta</td><td>din</td><td>|-</td><td>din</td><td>-</td><td>ta</td></tr>
<tr><td>|ta</td><td>din</td><td>-</td><td>din</td><td>|-</td><td>ta</td><td>ta</td><td>din</td><td>|-</td><td>din</td><td>-</td><td>ta</td></tr>
<tr><td colspan="12">Stage V+ mōrā 3</td></tr>
<tr><td>|ta</td><td>ka</td><td>di</td><td>mi</td><td>|ta</td><td>ka</td><td>ta</td><td>ki</td><td>|ṭa</td><td>(ta)</td><td>[tam</td><td>-</td></tr>
<tr><td>|-</td><td>-</td><td>-</td><td>-]</td><td>|(ta)</td><td>[tam</td><td>-</td><td>-</td><td>|-</td><td>-</td><td>-]</td><td>(ta)</td></tr>
</table>

04-042N

tiśra jāti ēka tāḷa

mōrā series 2, mōrā 4

I				•				•			
Stage III											
|**din**	-	ta	ta	|din	-	**ta**	din	|-	din	-	ta
|**din**	-	ta	ta	|din	-	**ta**	din	|-	din	-	ta
|**din**	-	ta	ta	|din	-	**ta**	din	|-	din	-	ta
|**din**	-	ta	ta	|din	-	**ta**	din	|-	din	-	ta
Stage IV											
|**ta**	din	-	din	|-	ta	**ta**	din	|-	din	-	ta
|**ta**	din	-	din	|-	ta	**ta**	din	|-	din	-	ta
Stage V+ mōrā 4											
|ta	ka	ta	ki	|ṭa	(ta)	[tam	-	|-	-	-	-
|-	-]	(ta)	[tam	|-	-	-	-	|-	-	-]	(ta)

04-043N

tiśra jāti ēka tāḷa

mōrā series 2, mōrā 5

|				•				•			
Stage III											
|**din**	-	ta	ta	|din	-	**ta**	din	|-	din	-	ta
|**din**	-	ta	ta	|din	-	**ta**	din	|-	din	-	ta
|**din**	-	ta	ta	|din	-	**ta**	din	|-	din	-	ta
|**din**	-	ta	ta	|din	-	**ta**	din	|-	din	-	ta
Stage IV											
|**ta**	din	-	din	|-	ta	**ta**	din	|-	din	-	ta
|**ta**	din	-	din	|-	ta	**ta**	din	|-	din	-	ta
Stage V+ mōrā 5											
|-	(ta)	[tam	-	|-	-	-	-	|-	-	-	-]
|(ta)	[tam	-	-	|-	-	-	-	|-	-	-]	(ta)

05-044N

tiśra jāti ēka tāḷa

exercise mōrā 1

<table>
<tr><td>|</td><td></td><td></td><td></td><td>•</td><td></td><td></td><td></td><td>•</td><td></td><td></td><td></td></tr>
<tr><td>|(ta</td><td>-</td><td>-</td><td>-</td><td>|ki</td><td>-</td><td>-</td><td>-</td><td>|ṭa</td><td>-</td><td>-</td><td>-</td></tr>
<tr><td>|ta</td><td>-</td><td>-</td><td>ki</td><td>|-</td><td>-</td><td>ṭa</td><td>-</td><td>|-</td><td>ta</td><td>-</td><td>ki</td></tr>
<tr><td>|-</td><td>ṭa</td><td>-</td><td>ta</td><td>|ki</td><td>ṭa)</td><td>[tām</td><td>-</td><td>|-]</td><td>(ta</td><td>-</td><td>-</td></tr>
<tr><td>|-</td><td>ki</td><td>-</td><td>-</td><td>|-</td><td>ṭa</td><td>-</td><td>-</td><td>|-</td><td>ta</td><td>-</td><td>-</td></tr>
<tr><td>|ki</td><td>-</td><td>-</td><td>ṭa</td><td>|-</td><td>-</td><td>ta</td><td>-</td><td>|ki</td><td>-</td><td>ṭa</td><td>-</td></tr>
<tr><td>|ta</td><td>ki</td><td>ṭa)</td><td>[tām</td><td>|-</td><td>-]</td><td>(ta</td><td>-</td><td>|-</td><td>-</td><td>ki</td><td>-</td></tr>
<tr><td>|-</td><td>-</td><td>ṭa</td><td>-</td><td>|-</td><td>-</td><td>ta</td><td>-</td><td>|-</td><td>ki</td><td>-</td><td>-</td></tr>
<tr><td>|ṭa</td><td>-</td><td>-</td><td>ta</td><td>|-</td><td>ki</td><td>-</td><td>ṭa</td><td>|-</td><td>ta</td><td>ki</td><td>ṭa)</td></tr>
</table>

tām

05-052N

exercise mōrā 2

khaṇḍa jāti ēka tāḷa

<table>
<tr><th colspan="4">| clap</th><th colspan="4">• pinky</th><th colspan="4">• ring</th><th colspan="4">• middle</th><th colspan="4">• index</th></tr>
<tr><td>|(ta</td><td>-</td><td>-</td><td>-</td><td>|ka</td><td>-</td><td>-</td><td>-</td><td>|ta</td><td>-</td><td>-</td><td>-</td><td>|ki</td><td>-</td><td>-</td><td>-</td><td>|ṭa</td><td>-</td><td>-</td><td>-</td></tr>
<tr><td>|ta</td><td>-</td><td>-</td><td>ka</td><td>|-</td><td>-</td><td>ta</td><td>-</td><td>|-</td><td>ki</td><td>-</td><td>-</td><td>|ṭa</td><td>-</td><td>-</td><td>ta</td><td>|-</td><td>ka</td><td>-</td><td>ta</td></tr>
<tr><td>|-</td><td>ki</td><td>-</td><td>ṭa</td><td>|-</td><td>ta</td><td>ka</td><td>ta</td><td>|ki</td><td>ṭa)</td><td>[tām</td><td>-</td><td>|-</td><td>-</td><td>-]</td><td>(ta</td><td>|-</td><td>-</td><td>-</td><td>ka</td></tr>
<tr><td>|-</td><td>-</td><td>-</td><td>ta</td><td>|-</td><td>-</td><td>-</td><td>ki</td><td>|-</td><td>-</td><td>-</td><td>ṭa</td><td>|-</td><td>-</td><td>-</td><td>ta</td><td>|-</td><td>-</td><td>ka</td><td>-</td></tr>
<tr><td>|-</td><td>ta</td><td>-</td><td>-</td><td>|ki</td><td>-</td><td>-</td><td>ṭa</td><td>|-</td><td>-</td><td>ta</td><td>-</td><td>|ka</td><td>-</td><td>ta</td><td>-</td><td>|ki</td><td>-</td><td>ṭa</td><td>-</td></tr>
<tr><td>|ta</td><td>ka</td><td>ta</td><td>ki</td><td>|ṭa)</td><td>[tām</td><td>-</td><td>-</td><td>|-</td><td>-]</td><td>(ta</td><td>-</td><td>|-</td><td>-</td><td>ka</td><td>-</td><td>|-</td><td>-</td><td>ta</td><td>-</td></tr>
<tr><td>|-</td><td>-</td><td>ki</td><td>-</td><td>|-</td><td>-</td><td>ṭa</td><td>-</td><td>|-</td><td>-</td><td>ta</td><td>-</td><td>|-</td><td>ka</td><td>-</td><td>-</td><td>|ta</td><td>-</td><td>-</td><td>ki</td></tr>
<tr><td>|-</td><td>-</td><td>ṭa</td><td>-</td><td>|-</td><td>ta</td><td>-</td><td>ka</td><td>|-</td><td>ta</td><td>-</td><td>ki</td><td>|-</td><td>ṭa</td><td>-</td><td>ta</td><td>|ka</td><td>ta</td><td>ki</td><td>ṭa)</td></tr>
</table>

05-060N

exercise mōrā 3

miśra jāti ēka tāḷa

clap	• pinky	• ring	• middle	• index	• thumb	• pinky
(ta - - -	ka - - -	di - - -	mi - - -	ta - - -	ki - - -	ṭa - - -
ta - - ka	- - di -	- mi - -	ta - - ki	- - ṭa -	- ta - ka	- di - mi
- ta - ki	- ṭa - ta	ka di mi ta	ki ṭa) [tām -	- - - -	-] (ta - -	- ka - -
- di - -	- mi - -	- ta - -	- ki - -	- ṭa - -	- ta - -	ka - - di
- - mi -	- ta - -	ki - - ṭa	- - ta -	ka - di -	mi - ta -	ki - ṭa -
ta ka di mi	ta ki ṭa) [tām	- - - -	- -] (ta -	- - ka -	- - di -	- - mi -
- - ta -	- - ki -	- - ṭa -	- - ta -	- ka - -	di - - mi	- - ta -
- ki - -	ṭa - - ta	- ka - di	- mi - ta	- ki - ṭa	- ta ka di	mi ta ki ṭa)

05-068N

śaṅkīrna jāti ēka tāḷa

exercise mōrā 4

• clap	• pinky	• ring	• middle	• index	• thumb	• pinky	• ring	• middle
(ta- - -	ka - - -	di - - -	mi- - -	ta - - -	ka - - -	ta - - -	ki - - -	ṭa - - -
ta - - ka	- - di -	- mi- -	ta - - ka	- - ta -	- ki - -	ṭa - - ta	- ka - di	- mi - ta
- ka - ta	- ki - ṭa	- ta ka di	mi ta ka ta	ki ṭa [tām-	- - - -	- - -] (ta	- - - ka	- - - di
- - - mi	- - - ta	- - - ka	- - - ta	- - - ki	- - - ṭa	- - - ta	- - ka -	- di - -
mi - - ta	- - ka -	- ta - -	ki - - ṭa	- - ta -	ka - di -	mi - ta -	ka - ta -	ki - ṭa -
ta ka di mi	ta ka ta ki	ṭa [tām- -	- - - -	- -] (ta-	- - ka -	- - di -	- - mi-	- - ta -
- - ka -	- - ta -	- - ki -	- - ṭa -	- - ta -	- ka - -	di - - mi	- - ta -	- ka - -
ta - - ki	- - ṭa -	- ta - ka	- di - mi	- ta - ka	- ta - ki	- ṭa - ta	ka di mi ta	ka ta ki ṭa

ādi tāḷa

06-073N
ādi mōrā 1

| clap	• pinky	• ring	• middle	O clap	• wave	O clap	• wave
Stage I							
a: ta - din -	din - na -	b: ta ka din -	din - na -	c: - - din -	din - na -	d: kṭ tk din -	din - na -
a: ta - din -	din - na -	b: ta ka din -	din - na -	c: - - din -	din - na -	e: - - ta ta	kṭ tom tom ta
a: ta - din -	din - na -	b: ta ka din -	din - na -	c: - - din -	din - na -	d: kṭ tk din -	din - na -
a: ta - din -	din - na -	b: ta ka din -	din - na -	c: - - din -	din - na -	e: - - ta ta	kṭ tom tom ta
Stage II							
a: ta - din -	din - na -	b: ta ka din -	din - na -	c: - - din -	din - na -	e: - - ta ta	kṭ tom tom ta
a: ta - din -	din - na -	b: ta ka din -	din - na -	c: - - din -	din - na -	e: - - ta ta	kṭ tom tom ta
Stage III							
a: ta - din -	din - na -	e: - - ta ta	kṭ tom tom ta	b: ta ka din -	din - na -	e: - - ta ta	kṭ tom tom ta
c: - - din -	din - na -	e: - - ta ta	kṭ tom tom ta	d: kṭ tk din -	din - na -	e: - - ta ta	kṭ tom tom ta
Stage IV							
a: ta - din -	din - na -	mōrā: (ta ta kṭ tom	tom ta) [tam -	-] (ta ta kṭ	tom tom ta) [tam	- -] (ta ta	kṭ tom tom ta)

06-076N
ādi mōrā 2

ādi tāḷa

| • • • O • O •

Stage III

a e b e
|ta - din - |din - na - |- - ta ta |kṭ tom tom ta |ta ka din - |din - na - |- - ta ta |kṭ tom tom ta

c e d e
|- - din - |din - na - |- - ta ta |kṭ tom tom ta |kṭ tk din - |din - na - |- - ta ta |kṭ tom tom ta

Stage IV

a mōrā
|ta - din - |din - na - |(ta ta kṭ tom|tom ta) [tām -] | (kṭ tom tom ta) |[tām -](tom tom|ta) [tām -] (tom|ta) [tam -] (ta)

06-077N
ādi mōrā 3

ādi tāḷa

| • • • O • O •

Stage III

a e b e
|ta - din - |din - na - |- - ta ta |kṭ tom tom ta |ta ka din - |din - na - |- - ta ta |kṭ tom tom ta

c e d e
|- - din - |din - na - |- - ta ta |kṭ tom tom ta |kṭ tk din - |din - na - |- - ta ta |kṭ tom tom ta

Stage IV

a mōrā
|ta - din - |din - na - |(ta) [tām -](tom|ta) [tam -](tom|tom ta) [tām -]|(kṭ tom tom ta) |[tām -] (ta ta |kṭ tom tom ta)

ādi tāḷa

06-078N
compound mōrā 1

I	•	•	•	O	•	O	•
Stage I							
a: ta - din -	din - na -	b: ta ka din -	din - na -	c: - - din -	din - na -	d: kṭ tk din -	din - na -
a: ta - din -	din - na -	b: ta ka din -	din - na -	c: - - din -	din - na -	e: - - ta ta	kṭ tom tom ta
a: ta - din -	din - na -	b: ta ka din -	din - na -	c: - - din -	din - na -	d: kṭ tk din -	din - na -
a: ta - din -	din - na -	b: ta ka din -	din - na -	c: - - din -	din - na -	e: - - ta ta	kṭ tom tom ta
Stage II							
a: ta - din -	din - na -	b: ta ka din -	din - na -	c: - - din -	din - na -	e: - - ta ta	kṭ tom tom ta
a: ta - din -	din - na -	b: ta ka din -	din - na -	c: - - din -	din - na -	e: - - ta ta	kṭ tom tom ta
Stage III							
a: ta - din -	din - na -	e: - - ta ta	kṭ tom tom ta	b: ta ka din -	din - na -	e: - - ta ta	kṭ tom tom ta
c: - - din -	din - na -	e: - - ta ta	kṭ tom tom ta	d: kṭ tk din -	din - na -	e: - - ta ta	kṭ tom tom ta
Stage IV							
a: ta - din -	din - na -	e: - - ta ta	kṭ tom tom ta	b: ta ka din -	din - na -	mōrā: (ta ta kṭ tom	tom ta) [tām -
-] (ta ta kṭ	tom tom ta) [tām	- -] (ta ta	kṭ tom tom ta)	(ta ta kṭ tom	tom ta) [tām -	-] (ta ta kṭ	tom tom ta) [tām
- -] (ta ta	kṭ tom tom ta)	(ta ta kṭ tom	tom ta) [tām -	-] (ta ta kṭ	tom tom ta) [tām	- -] (ta ta	kṭ to to ta)

06-079N
compound mōrā 2

ādi tāḷa

| • • • O • O •

Stage IV

a | e | b | mōrā

|ta - din - |din - na - |- - ta ta |kṭ tom tom ta | ta ka din - |din - na - |(ta ta kṭ tom|tom ta) [tām -]

|(kṭ tom tom ta) |[tām -] (tom tom| ta) [tām -] (tom |ta) [tām -] (ta) | (ta ta kṭ tom|tom ta) [tām -] | (kṭ tom tom ta) |[tām -] (tom tom

|ta) [tām -] (tom | ta) [tām -] (ta) | (ta ta kṭ tom |tom ta) [tām -] |(kṭ tom tom ta) |[tām -] (tom tom| ta) [tām -] (tom| ta) [tam -] (ta)

06-080N
compound mōrā 3

ādi tāḷa

| • • • O • O •

Stage IV

a | e | b | mōrā

|ta - din - |din - na - |- - ta ta |kṭ tom tom ta | ta ka din - |din - na - |(ta) [tām -] (tom|ta) [tām -] (tom

|tom ta) [tām -] |(kṭ tom tom ta) |[tām -] (ta ta |kṭ tom tom ta) |(ta) [tām -] (tom|ta) [tām -] (tom |tom ta) [tām -] |(kṭ tom tom ta)

| [tām -] (ta ta |kṭ tom tom ta) |(ta) [tām -] (tom|ta) [tām -] (tom |tom ta) [tām -] |(kṭ tom tom ta) |[tām -] (ta ta |kṭ tom tom ta)

06-081N
compound mōrā 4

ādi tāḷa

I	•	•	•	O	•	O	•
Stage IV						mōrā	
ta - din -	din - na -	- - ta ta	kṭ to to ta	ta - din -	din - na -	(ta ta kṭ tom	tom ta) [tām -]
(kṭ tom tom ta)	[tām -] (tom tom	ta) [tām -] (tom	ta) [tām -] (ta)	(ta ta kṭ tom	tom ta) [tām -	-] (ta ta kṭ	tom tom ta) [tām
- -] (ta ta	kṭ tom tom ta)	(ta) [tām -] (tom	ta) [tām -] (tom	tom ta) [tām -]	(kṭ tom tom ta)	[tām -] (ta ta	kṭ tom tom ta)

06-082N
compound mōrā 5

ādi tāḷa

I	•	•	•	O	•	O	•
Stage IV a		e		b		mōrā	
ta - din -	din - na -	- - ta ta	kṭ tom tom ta	ta ka din -	din - na -	(ta) [tām -] (tom	ta) [tām -] (tom
tom ta) [tām -]	(kṭ tom tom ta)	[tām -] (ta ta	kṭ tom tom ta)	(ta ta kṭ tom	tom ta) [tām -	-] (ta ta kṭ	tom tom ta) [tām
- -] (ta ta	kṭ tom tom ta)	(ta ta kṭ tom	tom ta) [tām -]	(kṭ tom tom ta)	[tām -] (tom tom	ta) [tām -] (tom	ta) [tām -] (ta)

07-085N

divisions of the cycle

ādi tāḷa

| • • • O • O •

two pulses per beat, two patterns per cycle

|**ta** ka |di mi |ta ka |jo ṇu |**ta** ka |di mi |ta ka |jo ṇu

three pulses per beat, three patterns per cycle

|**ta** ka di |mi ta ka |jo ṇu **ta** |ka di mi |ta ka jo |ṇu **ta** ka |di mi ta |ka jo ṇu

four pulses per beat, four patterns per cycle

|**ta** ka di mi |ta ka jo ṇu |**ta** ka di mi |ta ka jo ṇu |**ta** ka di mi |ta ka jo ṇu |**ta** ka di mi |ta ka jo ṇu

07-091N

ādi tāḷa

Palani Subramania Pillai composition in three speeds

I	•	•	•	O	•	O	•
original speed (4 pulses per beat)							
tām - - -	ta ka din -	din - din -	na - tr gḍ	tom ta ka tom	ta ka din -	tām - tām -	dī - - -
- - ki ṭa	ta ka din -	din - din -	na - tr gḍ	tom ta ka tom	ta ka din -	din na kṭ tk	tām - - -
tām - - -	ta ka din -	din - din -	na - tr gḍ	tom ta ka tom	ta ka din -	tām - tām -	dī - - -
- - ki ṭa	ta ka din -	din - din -	na - tr gḍ	tom ta ka tom	ta ka din -	din na kṭ tk	tām - - -
(tām- - -	ta ka di na	tom ta ka tom	ta ka di na	din na kṭ tk)	[tam -] (tām -	- - ta ka	di na tom ta
ka tom ta ka	di na din na	kṭ tk) [tam -]	(tām - - -	ta ka di na	tom ta ka tom	ta ka di na	dinna kṭ tk)
second speed (tiśram: 6 pulses per beat)							
tm - - - ta ka	dn - dn - dn -	na - ki ṭa to ta	ka to ta ka dn -	tm - tm - di -	- - - - ki ṭa	ta ka dn - dn -	dn - na - ki ṭa
to ta ka to ta ka	dn - ta ka jo ṇu	tm - - - tm -	- - ta ka dn -	dn - dn - na -	ki ṭa to ta ka to	ta ka dn - tm -	tm - di - - -
- - ki ṭa ta ka	dn - dn - dn -	na - ki ṭa to ta	ka to ta ka dn -	ta ka jo ṇu tm -	- - (tm - - -	ta ka di na to ta	ka to ta ka di na
ta ka jo ṇu [tm-]	(tm- - - ta ka	di na to ta ka to	ta ka di na ta ka	jo ṇu [tm -](tm -	- - ta ka di na	to ta ka to ta ka	di na ta ka jo ṇu)
third speed (8 pulses per beat)							
t - - - t k d -	d- d - n - k ṭ	t t k t t k d -	t - t - d - - -	- - k ṭ t k d -	d- d - n - k ṭ	t t k t t k d -	t k j ṇ t - - -
t - - - t k d -	d- d - n - k ṭ	t t k t t k d -	t - t - d - - -	- - k ṭ t k d -	d- d - n - k ṭ	t t k t t k d -	t k j ṇ t - - -
(t- - - t k d n	t t k t t k d n	t k j ṇ [t-](t-	- - t k d n t t	k t t k d n t k	j ṇ [t-](t- - -	t k d n t t k t	t k d n t k j ṇ

08-094N
kōrvai 1 with setup

ādi tāḷa

```
|                 •                 •                 •                 O                 •                 O                 •

Stage I
a                           b                           b                           b
|din  -  ta  na |ta  ta  jo  ṇu |jo  ṇu  ta  na |ta  ta  jo  ṇu |jo  ṇu  ta  na |ta  ta  jo  ṇu |jo  ṇu  ta  na |ta  ta  jo  ṇu

a                           b                           c                 phrase
|din  -  ta  na |ta  ta  jo  ṇu |jo  ṇu  ta  na |ta  ta  jo  ṇu |din  -  ta  ta |jo  ṇu  ta  ki |ṭa  tom -  ta |din gi  ṇa  tom

a                           b                           b                           b
|din  -  ta  na |ta  ta  jo  ṇu |jo  ṇu  ta  na |ta  ta  jo  ṇu |jo  ṇu  ta  na |ta  ta  jo  ṇu |jo  ṇu  ta  na |ta  ta  jo  ṇu

a                           b                           d                 phrase
|din  -  ta  na |ta  ta  jo  ṇu |jo  ṇu  ta  na |ta  ta  jo  ṇu |jo  ṇu  ta  ta |jo  ṇu  ta  ki |ṭa  tom -  ta |din gi  ṇa  tom

Stage II
a                           b                           c                 phrase
|din  -  ta  na |ta  ta  jo  ṇu |jo  ṇu  ta  na |ta  ta  jo  ṇu |din  -  ta  ta |jo  ṇu  ta  ki |ṭa  tom -  ta |din gi  ṇa  tom

a                           b                           d                 phrase
|din  -  ta  na |ta  ta  jo  ṇu |jo  ṇu  ta  na |ta  ta  jo  ṇu |jo  ṇu  ta  ta |jo  ṇu  ta  ki |ṭa  tom -  ta |din gi  ṇa  tom

Stage III
c                 phrase                              d                 phrase
|din  -  ta  ta |jo  ṇu  ta  ki |ṭa  tom -  ta |din gi  ṇa  tom|jo  ṇu  ta  ta |jo  ṇu  ta  ki |ṭa  tom -  ta |din gi  ṇa  tom

c                 phrase                              d                 phrase
|din  -  ta  ta |jo  ṇu  ta  ki |ṭa  tom -  ta |din gi  ṇa  tom|jo  ṇu  ta  ta |jo  ṇu  ta  ki |ṭa  tom -  ta |din gi  ṇa  tom

kōrvai
A                                   B         C           D       A                                           B
|ta  ki  ṭa  tom|-  ta  din gi |ṇa  tom jo  ṇu |jo  ṇu  tom - |ta  -  tām - |-  ta  ki  ṭa |tom -  ta  din |gi  ṇa  tom jo

            C             D             A                                     B               C              D          B
|ṇu  jo  ṇu  tom|-  ta  -  tām |-  -  ta  ki |ṭa  tom -  ta |din gi  ṇa  tom|jo  ṇu  jo  ṇu |tom -  ta  - |tām -  -  jo

            C             D             B               C            D           C              D             C
|ṇu  jo  ṇu  tom|-  ta  -  tām |-  -  jo  ṇu |jo  ṇu  (tom - |ta  -)  [tām - |-]  (tom-  ta |-)  [tām -  -] |(tom-  ta  -)
```

08-095N

kōrvai 1, variation 1

ādi tāḷa

```
I            •            •            •            O            •            O            •
A                                      B            C            D          A                                   B
|ta  ki  ṭa  tom|-  ta  din gi  |ṇa  tom jo  ṇu  |jo  ṇu  tom -  |ta  -  tām -  |-  ta  ki  ṭa  |tom -  ta  din |gi  ṇa  tom jo
             C            D            A                                 B            C            D          B
|ṇu  jo  ṇu  tom|-  ta  -  tām |-  -  ta  ki  |ṭa  tom -  ta  |din gi  ṇa  tom|jo  ṇu  jo  ṇu  |tom -  ta  -  |tām -  -  jo
             C            D            B                 C2        D           C4           D           C6
|ṇu  jo  ṇu  tom|-  ta  -  tām |-  -  jo  ṇu  |jo  ṇu  (tom ta)|[tām -  -](tom |-  ta  -)  [tām |-  -]  (tom  -  |  -  ta  -  - )
```

08-096N

kōrvai 1, variation 2

ādi tāḷa

```
I            •            •            •            O            •            O            •
A                                      B            C            D          A                                   B
|ta  ki  ṭa  tom|-  ta  din gi  |ṇa  tom jo  ṇu  |jo  ṇu  tom -  |ta  -  tām -  |-  ta  ki  ṭa  |tom -  ta  din |gi  ṇa  tom jo
             C            D            A                                 B            C            D          B
|ṇu  jo  ṇu  tom|-  ta  -  tām |-  -  ta  ki  |ṭa  tom -  ta  |din gi  ṇa  tom|jo  ṇu  jo  ṇu  |tom -  ta  -  |tām -  -  jo
             C            D            B                  C6                     D           C4           D           C2
|ṇu  jo  ṇu  tom|-  ta  -  tām |-  -  jo  ṇu  |jo  ṇu  (tom -|  -  ta  -  - )  |[tām -  -](tom|  -  ta  -)  [tām |  -  -](tom ta)
```

08-097N
kōrvai 1, variation 3

ādi tāḷa

| • • • O • O •

A B C2 D A B
|ta ki ṭa tom| - ta din gi |ṇa tom jo ṇu |jo ṇu tom ta |tām - - ta| ki ṭa tom - | ta din gi ṇa |tom jo ṇu jo

C4 D A B C6 D B
|ṇu tom - ta | - tām - - |ta ki ṭa tom| - ta din gi| ṇa tom jo ṇu |jo ṇu tom - | - ta - - |tām - - jo

C4 D B C2 D C4 D C6
|ṇu jo ṇu tom| - ta - tām|- - jo ṇu |jo ṇu (tom ta)|[tām - -](tom| - ta -) [tām |- -] (tom - | - ta - -)

08-098N
kōrvai 1, variation 4

ādi tāḷa

| • • • O • O •

A B C6 A
|ta ki ṭa tom| - ta din gi |ṇa tom jo ṇu |jo ṇu tom - | - ta - - | tām - - ta |ki ṭa tom - |ta din gi ṇa

B C4 D A B C2 D B
| tom jo ṇu jo| ṇu tom - ta | - tām - - |ta ki ṭa tom| - ta din gi |ṇa tom jo ṇu | jo ṇu tom ta |tām - - jo

C4 D B C6 D C4 D C2
|ṇu jo ṇu tom| - ta - tām|- - jo ṇu |jo ṇu (tom -| - ta - -) |[tām - -](tom| - ta -) [tām | - -](tom ta)

ādi tāḷa

08-101N
kōrvai 1, variation 5

| • • • O • O •

Stage I

a b b b
|din - ta na |ta ta jo ṇu |jo ṇu ta na |ta ta jo ṇu |jo ṇu ta na |ta ta jo ṇu |jo ṇu ta na |ta ta jo ṇu

a b c phrase
|din - ta na |ta ta jo ṇu |jo ṇu ta na |ta ta jo ṇu |din - ta ta |jo ṇu ta - | tr gg tr gḍ |dk tk tr gḍ

a b b b
|din - ta na |ta ta jo ṇu |jo ṇu ta na |ta ta jo ṇu |jo ṇu ta na |ta ta jo ṇu |jo ṇu ta na |ta ta jo ṇu

a b d phrase
|din - ta na |ta ta jo ṇu |jo ṇu ta na |ta ta jo ṇu |jo ṇu ta ta |jo ṇu ta - | tr gg tr gḍ |dk tk tr gḍ

Stage II

a b c phrase
|din - ta na |ta ta jo ṇu |jo ṇu ta na |ta ta jo ṇu |din - ta ta |jo ṇu ta - | tr gg tr gḍ |dk tk tr gḍ

a b d phrase
|din - ta na |ta ta jo ṇu |jo ṇu ta na |ta ta jo ṇu |jo ṇu ta ta |jo ṇu ta - | tr gg tr gḍ |dk tk tr gḍ

Stage III

c phrase d phrase
|din - ta ta |jo ṇu ta - | tr gg tr gḍ |dk tk tr gḍ |jo ṇu ta ta |jo ṇu ta - | tr gg tr gḍ |dk tk tr gḍ

c phrase d phrase
|din - ta ta |jo ṇu ta - | tr gg tr gḍ |dk tk tr gḍ |jo ṇu ta ta |jo ṇu ta - | tr gg tr gḍ |dk tk tr gḍ

kōrvai

|A B C D A B
ta - tr gg |tr gḍ dk tk |tr gḍ tr gḍ | ta - tom - |ta - tām - |- ta - tr |gg tr gḍ dk |tk tr gḍ tr

| C D A B C D B
gḍ ta - tom|- ta - tām|- - ta - | tr gg tr gḍ |dk tk tr gḍ |tr gḍ ta - |tom - ta - |tām - - tr

| C D B C D C D C
gḍ ta - tom|- ta - tām |- - tr gḍ | ta - (tom - |ta -) [tām - |-] (tom - ta |-) [tām - -] |(tom - ta -)

08-102N
kōrvai 1, variation 6

ādi tāḷa

I • • • O • O •

A B C D A B
|ta - tr gg |tr gḍ dk tk |tr gḍ tr gḍ | ta - tom - |ta - tām - |- ta - tr |gg tr gḍ dk |tk tr gḍ tr

C D A B C D B
|gḍ ta - tom|- ta - tām |- - ta - | tr gg tr gḍ |dk tk tr gḍ |tr gḍ ta - |tom - ta - |tām - - tr

C D B C2 D C4 D C6
|gḍ ta - tom|- ta - tām |- - tr gḍ | ta - (tom ta)|[tām - -](tom | - ta -) [tām | - -] (tom - | - ta - -)

08-103N
kōrvai 1, variation 7

ādi tāḷa

I • • • O • O •

A B C D A B
|ta - tr gg |tr gḍ dk tk |tr gḍ tr gḍ | ta - tom - |ta - tām - |- ta - tr |gg tr gḍ dk |tk tr gḍ tr

C D A B C D B
|gḍ ta - tom|- ta - tām |- - ta - | tr gg tr gḍ |dk tk tr gḍ |tr gḍ ta - |tom - ta - |tām - - tr

C D B C6 D C4 D C2
|gḍ ta - tom|- ta - tām |- - tr gḍ | ta - (tom -| - ta - -) |[tām - -](tom| - ta -) [tām | - -] (tom ta)

08-104N

kōrvai 1, variation 8

ādi tāḷa

```
I                 •                 •                 •                 O                 •                 O                 •
A                                              B                 C2        D                A
|ta  -  tr  gg |tr  gḍ  dk  tk |tr  gḍ  tr  gḍ | ta  -  tom  ta | tām  -   -  ta |-  tr  gg  tr |gḍ  dk  tk  tr |gḍ  tr  gḍ  ta
                                                                                                                    B
   C4              D         A                                B         C6                             D           B
| -  tom  -  ta |-  tām  -  - |ta  -  tr  gg| tr  gḍ  dk  tk |tr  gḍ  tr  gḍ |ta  -  tom  - | -  ta  -  - |tām  -  -  tr
         C4           D               B           C2       D          C4             D           C6
|gḍ  ta  -  tom|-  ta  -  tām |-  -  tr  gḍ | ta  -  (tom ta)|[tām -  -](tom |- ta  -)  [tām |-  -]  (tom - | - ta  -  - )
```

08-105N

kōrvai 1, variation 9

ādi tāḷa

```
I                 •                 •                 •                 O                 •                 O                 •
A                                              B         C6                              D          A
|ta  -  tr  gg |tr  gḍ  dk  tk |tr  gḍ  tr  gḍ | ta  -  tom  - |  -  ta  -  - |tām  -  -  ta |-  tr  gg  tr |gḍ  dk  tk  tr
    B              C4            D        A                               B                C2     D            B
| gḍ  tr  gḍ  ta |-  tom  -  ta |-  tām  -  - |ta  -  tr  gg| tr  gḍ  dk  tk |tr  gḍ  tr  gḍ| ta  -  tom  ta|tām  -  -  tr
         C4           D               B              C6                   D           C4           D              C2
|gḍ  ta  -  tom|-  ta  -  tām |-  -  tr  gḍ | ta  -  (tom -|  -  ta  -  - ) |[tām -  -](tom| - ta  -)  [tām | -  -](tom ta)
```

ādi tāḷa

09-106N
tiśra kōrvai setup

I	•	•	•	O	•	O	•
Stage I							
a		b		a		c	
|din - ta	|ta din -	|- - ta	|ta din -	|din - ta	|ta din -	|ta na ta	|ta din -
a		b		i			
|din - ta	|ta din -	|- - ta	|ta din -	|ta di -	|ta tom -	|- ta di	|ki ṭa tom
a		b		a		c	
|din - ta	|ta din -	|- - ta	|ta din -	|din - ta	|ta din -	|ta na ta	|ta din -
a		b		ii			
|din - ta	|ta din -	|- - ta	|ta din -	|- di -	|ta tom -	|- ta di	|ki ṭa tom
a		b		a		c	
|din - ta	|ta din -	|- - ta	|ta din -	|din - ta	|ta din -	|ta na ta	|ta din -
a		b		iii			
|din - ta	|ta din -	|- - ta	|ta din -	|- - -	|ta tom -	|- ta di	|ki ṭa tom
Stage II							
a		b		i			
|din - ta	|ta din -	|- - ta	|ta din -	|ta di -	|ta tom -	|- ta di	|ki ṭa tom
a		b		ii			
|din - ta	|ta din -	|- - ta	|ta din -	|- di -	|ta tom -	|- ta di	|ki ṭa tom
a		b		iii			
|din - ta	|ta din -	|- - ta	|ta din -	|- - -	|ta tom -	|- ta di	|ki ṭa tom
Stage III							
i				ii			
|ta di -	|ta tom -	|- ta di	|ki ṭa tom	|- di -	|ta tom -	|- ta di	|ki ṭa tom
iii				i			
|- - -	|ta tom -	|- ta di	|ki ṭa tom	|ta di -	|ta tom -	|- ta di	|ki ṭa tom
ii				iii			
|- di -	|ta tom -	|- ta di	|ki ṭa tom	|- - -	|ta tom -	|- ta di	|ki ṭa tom

09-107N
tiśra kōrvai original

ādi tāḷa

```
|        •        •        •        O        •        O        •
|ta  di  -  |ta  tōm -  | -  ta  di  | ki  ṭa  tom |  tām -  - | di  -  ta  | tōm -  - | ta  di  ki
|ṭa  tom  tām | -  -  ta |  tōm -  - |(ta  di  ki  |ṭa  tom) (ta  |di  ki  ṭa  |tom) (ta  di  |ki  ṭa  tom)
```

09-108N
tiśra kōrvai variation 1

ādi tāḷa

```
|        •        •        •        O        •        O        •
|ta  di  -  |ta  tōm -  |-  ta  di  |ki  ṭa  tom |di  -  ta  |tōm -  -  |ta  di  ki  |ṭa  tom  ta
|tōm -  -  |(ta  di  ki  |ṭa  tom) [tām| -  -]  (ta  |di  ki  ṭa  |tom) [tām -  |-]  (ta  di  |ki  ṭa  tom)
```

09-109N
tiśra kōrvai variation 2

ādi tāḷa

```
|        •        •        •        O        •        O        •
|ta  di  -  |ta  tōm -  |-  ta  di  |ki  ṭa  tom |tām -  di  |-  ta  tōm |-  -  ta  |di  ki  ṭa
|tom  tām -  |ta  tōm -  |-  (ta  di  |ki  ṭa  tom)|[-]  (ta  di  |ki  ṭa  tom)|[-]  (ta  di  |ki  ṭa  tom)
```

09-110N
tiśra kōrvai variation 3

ādi tāḷa

I • • • O • O •

|ta di - |ta tōm - |- ta di |ki ṭa tōm |- di - |ta tōm - |- ta di |ki ṭa tōm
|- ta tōm |- - (ta |di ki ṭa |tom) [tām -] |(ta di ki |ṭa tom)[tām|-] (ta di |ki ṭa tom)

09-111N
tiśra kōrvai 1 alternate

ādi tāḷa

I • • • O • O •

|ta di - |ta tōm - | - ta di | ki ṭa tom | - - - | di - ta | tōm - - | ta di ki
|ṭa tom - | - - ta | tōm - - |(ta di ki |ṭa tom) (ta |di ki ṭa |tom) (ta di |ki ṭa tom)

09-112N
tiśra kōrvai variation 4

ādi tāḷa

I • • • O • O •

|ta di - |ta tōm - |- ta di |ki ṭa tom |di - ta |tōm - - |ta di ki |ṭa tom ta
|tōm - - |(ta di ki |ṭa tom) [- | - -] (ta |di ki ṭa |tom) [- - |-] (ta di |ki ṭa tom)

09-113N
tiśra kōrvai variation 5

ādi tāḷa

I • • • O • O •

|ta di - |ta tōm - |- ta di |ki ṭa tōm |- - di |- ta tōm |- - ta |di ki ṭa

|tōm - - |ta tōm - |- (ta di |ki ṭa tom) |[-] (ta di |ki ṭa tom) |[-] (ta di |ki ṭa tom)

09-114N
tiśra kōrvai variation 6

ādi tāḷa

I • • • O • O •

|ta di - |ta tōm - |- ta di |ki ṭa tōm |- di - |ta tōm - |- ta di |ki ṭa tōm

|- ta tōm |- - (ta |di ki ṭa |tōm) [- -] |(ta di ki |ṭa tōm) [- |-] (ta di |ki ṭa tom)

ādi tāḷa

10-117N
miśra koraippu stage I, pattern 1

I	•	•	•	O	•	O	•
tām - - -	- - - -	**ta** ka di mi	ta ki ṭa **ta**	ka di mi ta	ki ṭa **ta** ka	di mi ta ki	ṭa **ta** ka di
mi ta ki ṭa	**ta** ka di mi	ta ki ṭa **ta**	ka di mi ta	ki ṭa **ta** ka	di mi ta ki	ṭa **ta** ka di	mi ta ki ṭa

ādi tāḷa

10-118N
miśra koraippu stage I, pattern 2

I	•	•	•	O	•	O	•
tām - - -	- - - -	**ta** - din -	ta din - **ta**	ka din - ta	din - **ta** -	din - ta din	- **ta** - din
- gi ṇa tom	**ta** - din -	ta din - (ta	- din - gi	ṇa tom) (ta -	din - gi ṇa	tom) (ta - din	- gi ṇa tom)

ādi tāḷa

10-119N
miśra koraippu stage I, pattern 3

I	•	•	•	O	•	O	•
tām - - -	- - - -	**ta** - din -	ta din - **ta**	ka din - ta	din - **ta** -	din - ta din	- **ta** - din
- gi ṇa tom	**ta** - din -	ta din - (ta	din gi ṇa tom)	(ta - din -	gi ṇa tom) (ta	- din - gi	- ṇa - tom)

10-120N
miśra koraippu stage I, pattern 4

ādi tāḷa

I	•	•	•	O	•	O	•
tām - - -	- - - -	**ta** - din -	ta din - **ta**	ka din - ta	din - **ta** -	din - ta din	- **ta** - din
- gi ṇa tom	**ta** - din -	ta din - (ta	- din - gi	- ṇa - tom)	(ta - din -	gi ṇa tom)(ta	din gi ṇa tom)

10-121N
miśra koraippu stage I, pattern 5

ādi tāḷa

I	•	•	•	O	•	O	•
tām - - -	- - - -	**ta** ka di mi	ta ki ṭa **ta**	ka di mi ta	ki ṭa **ta** ka	di mi ta ki	ṭa **ta** ka di
mi ta ki ṭa	tiśram (ta ka di	mi ta ki	ṭa) (ta ka	di mi ta	ki ṭa) (ta	ka di mi	ta ki ṭa)

10-122N
miśra koraippu stage I, pattern 6

ādi tāḷa

I	•	•	•	O	•	O	•
tām - - -	- - - -	**ta** - din -	ta din - **ta**	ka din - ta	din - **ta** -	din - ta din	- **ta** - din
- gi ṇa tom	tiśram (ta - din	- gi ṇa	tom) (ta -	din - gi	ṇa tom) (ta	- din -	gi ṇa tom)

ādi tāḷa

10-123N
miśra koraippu stage I, pattern 7

I • • • O • O •

|tām - - - |- - - - |**ta** - din - |ta din - **ta** |ka din - ta |din - **ta** - |din - ta din |- **ta** - din

tiśram
|- gi ṇa tom| (ta din gi | ṇa tom) (ta | - din - |gi ṇa tom)| (ta - din | - gi - |ṇa - tom)

ādi tāḷa

10-124N
miśra koraippu stage I, pattern 8

I • • • O • O •

|tām - - - |- - - - |**ta** - din - |ta din - **ta** |ka din - ta |din - **ta** - |din - ta din |- **ta** - din

tiśram
|- gi ṇa tom| (ta - din | - gi - | ṇa - tom)| (ta - din | - gi ṇa | tom) (ta din |gi ṇa tom)

ādi tāḷa

10-125N
miśra koraippu stage I, pattern 9

I • • • O • O •

|tām - - - |- - - - |**ta** - din - |ta din - **ta** |ka din - ta |din - **ta** - |din - ta din |- **ta** - kṭ

| tk tr kṭ tom|**ta** - din - |ta din - (ta |- kṭ tk tr |kṭ tom) (ta - | kṭ tk tr kṭ |tom) (ta - kṭ |tk tr kṭ tom)

ādi tāḷa

10-126N
miśra koraippu stage I, pattern 10

I • • • O • O •

|tām - - - |- - - - |**ta** - din - |ta din - **ta** |ka din - ta |din - **ta** - |din - ta din |- **ta** - kṭ

| tk tr kṭ tom|**ta** - din - |ta din - (kṭ |tk tr kṭ tom)|(ta - kṭ tk | tr kṭ tom) (ta| - di - kṭ |tk tr kṭ tom)

ādi tāḷa

10-127N
miśra koraippu stage I, pattern 11

I • • • O • O •

|tām - - - |- - - - |**ta** - din - |ta din - **ta** |ka din - ta |din - **ta** - |din - ta din |- **ta** - kṭ

| tk tr kṭ tom|**ta** - din - |ta din - (ta |- di - kṭ |tk tr kṭ tom)| (ta - kṭ tk | tr kṭ tom) (kṭ |tk tr kṭ tom)

ādi tāḷa

10-128N
miśra koraippu stage I, pattern 12

I • • • O • O •

|tām - - - |- - - - |**ta** - din - |ta din - **ta** |ka din - ta |din - **ta** - |din - ta din |- **ta** - din

tiśram

|- gi ṇa tom| (ta - kṭ | tk tr kṭ | tom) (ta - | kṭ tk tr | kṭ tom) (ta | - kṭ tk | tr kṭ tom)

10-129N

ādi tāḷa

miśra koraippu stage I, pattern 13

| • • • O • O •

|tām - - - |- - - - |**ta** - din - |ta din - **ta** |ka din - ta |din - **ta** - |din - ta din |- **ta** - din

tiśram

|- gi ṇa tom| (kṭ tk tr | kṭ tom) (ta | - kṭ tk | tr kṭ tom) | (ta - di | - kṭ tk | tr kṭ tom)

10-130N

ādi tāḷa

miśra koraippu stage I, pattern 14

| • • • O • O •

|tām - - - |- - - - |**ta** - din - |ta din - **ta** |ka din - ta |din - **ta** - |din - ta din |- **ta** - din

tiśram

|- gi ṇa tom| (ta - di | - kṭ tk | tr kṭ tom) | (ta - kṭ | tk tr kṭ | tom) (kṭ tk | tr kṭ tom)

10-131N

ādi tāḷa

miśra koraippu stage II, pattern 1

| • • • O • O •

|tām - - - |**ta** ka di mi |ta ki ṭa **ta** |ka di mi ta |ki ṭa **ta** ka |di mi ta ki |ṭa **ta** ka di |mi ta ki ṭa

10-132N

ādi tāḷa — miśra koraippu stage II, pattern 2

| • • • O • O •

| tām - - - |**ta** - din - |ta din - (ta |- din - gi |ṇa tom) (ta - |din - gi ṇa |tom) (ta - din |- gi ṇa tom)

10-133N

ādi tāḷa — miśra koraippu stage II, pattern 3

| • • • O • O •

| tām - - - |**ta** - din - |ta din - (ta |din gi ṇa tom)|(ta - din - |gi ṇa tom) (ta | - din - gi | - ṇa - tom)

10-134N

ādi tāḷa — miśra koraippu stage II, pattern 4

| • • • O • O •

| tām - - - |**ta** - din - |ta din - (ta |- din - gi |- ṇa - tom)|(ta - din - |gi ṇa tom)(ta |din gi ṇa tom)

10-135N

ādi tāḷa — miśra koraippu stage II, pattern 5

I	•	•	•	O	•	O	•
	tiśram						
tām - - -	(ta ka di	mi ta ki	ṭa) (ta ka	di mi ta	ki ṭa) (ta	ka di mi	ta ki ṭa)

10-136N

ādi tāḷa — miśra koraippu stage II, pattern 6

I	•	•	•	O	•	O	•
	tiśram						
tām - - -	(ta - din	- gi ṇa	tom) (ta -	din - gi	ṇa tom) (ta	- din -	gi ṇa tom)

10-137N

ādi tāḷa — miśra koraippu stage II, pattern 7

I	•	•	•	O	•	O	•
	tiśram						
tām - - -	(ta din gi	ṇa tom) (ta	- din -	gi ṇa tom)	(ta - din	- gi -	ṇa - tom)

10-138N

ādi tāḷa

miśra koraippu stage II, pattern 8

I • • • O • O •

tiśram

| tām - - - | (ta - din | - gi - | ṇa - tom) | (ta - din | - gi ṇa | tom) (ta din | gi ṇa tom)

10-139N

ādi tāḷa

miśra koraippu stage II, pattern 9

I • • • O • O •

| tām - - - | **ta** - din - | ta din - (ta | - kṭ tk tr | kṭ tom) (ta - | kṭ tk tr kṭ | tom) (ta - kṭ | tk tr kṭ tom)

10-140N

ādi tāḷa

miśra koraippu stage II, pattern 10

I • • • O • O •

| tām - - - | **ta** - din - | ta din - (kṭ | tk tr kṭ tom) | (ta - kṭ tk | tr kṭ tom) (ta | - di - kṭ | tk tr kṭ tom)

10-141N

ādi tāḷa   miśra koraippu stage II, pattern 11

I • • • O • O •

|tām - - - |**ta** - din - |ta din - (ta| - di - kṭ |tk tr kṭ tom)|(ta - kṭ tk | tr kṭ tom) (kṭ| tk tr kṭ tom)

10-142N

ādi tāḷa   miśra koraippu stage II, pattern 12

I • • • O • O •

tiśram

| tām - - - |(ta - kṭ | tk tr kṭ | tom) (ta - | kṭ tk tr | kṭ tom) (ta | - kṭ tk | tr kṭ tom)

10-143N

ādi tāḷa   miśra koraippu stage II, pattern 13

I • • • O • O •

tiśram

| tām - - - |(kṭ tk tr | kṭ tom) (ta | - kṭ tk | tr kṭ tom) | (ta - di | - kṭ tk | tr kṭ tom)

10-144N

miśra koraippu stage II, pattern 14

ādi tāḷa

I	•	•	•	O	•	O	•
tāṃ - - -	tiśram (ta - di	- kṭ tk	tr kṭ tom)	(ta - kṭ	tk tr kṭ	tom) (kṭ tk	tr kṭ tom)

10-145N

miśra koraippu stage III

ādi tāḷa

I	•	•	•	O	•	O	•
tāṃ - **ta** ka	di mi ta ki	ṭa **ta** ka di	mi ta ki ṭa	tāṃ - **ta** -	din - ta din	- **ta** - din	- gi ṇa tom
tāṃ - **ta** ka	din - ta din	- **ta** - din	- gi ṇa tom	tāṃ - **ta** -	din - ta din	- **ta** di kṭ	tk tr kṭ tom

10-146N

miśra koraippu stage IV

ādi tāḷa

I	•	•	•	O	•	O	•
- **ta** - din	- gi ṇa tom	- **ta** - din	- gi ṇa tom	- **ta** - din	- gi ṇa tom	- **ta** - din	- gi ṇa tom

10-147N

miśra koraippu unison reduction

ādi tāḷa

I	•	•	•	O	•	O	•
seven							*six*
ta - din -	gi ṇa tom ta	- din - gi	ṇa tom ta -	din - gi ṇa	tom ta - din	- gi ṇa tom	ta din - gi
					five		
ṇa tom ta din	- gi ṇa tom	ta din - gi	ṇa tom ta din	- gi ṇa tom	ta din gi ṇa	tom ta din gi	ṇa tom ta din
		four				*three*	
gi ṇa tom ta	din gi ṇa tom	din gi ṇa tom	din gi ṇa tom	din gi ṇa tom	din gi ṇa tom	gi ṇa tom gi	ṇa tom gi ṇa
	two		*one*	mōrā			
tom gi ṇa tom	ṇa tom ṇa tom	ṇa tom ṇa tom	tom tom tom tom	tom (ta) [tām -	- - - -]	(ta) [tām - -	- - -] (ta)

ādi tāḷa

11-148N
ending section: preparation

I	•	•	•	O	•	O	•
Stage I							
a		a		a		b	
tām - - di	ta ka jo ṇu	tām - - di	ta ka jo ṇu	tām - - di	ta ka jo ṇu	tam tam tam di	ta ka jo ṇu
a		a		a		b	
tām - - di	ta ka jo ṇu	tām - - di	ta ka jo ṇu	tām - - di	ta ka jo ṇu	tam tam tam di	ta ka jo ṇu
a		b		a		b	
tām - - di	ta ka jo ṇu	tam tam tam di	ta ka jo ṇu	tām - - di	ta ka jo ṇu	tam tam tam di	ta ka jo ṇu
a		b		a		b	
tām - - di	ta ka jo ṇu	tam tam tam di	ta ka jo ṇu	tām - - di	ta ka jo ṇu	tam tam tam di	ta ka jo ṇu
a		b		mōrā			
tam tam tam di	ta ka jo ṇu	tam tam tam di	ta ka jo ṇu	(ta ka jo ṇu)	[tām -] (ta ka	jo ṇu) [tām -]	(ta ka jo ṇu)
Stage II							
a	a		a	a		c	d
tām - - ta	ki ṭa tām -	- ta ki ṭa	tām - - ta	ki ṭa tām -	- ta ki ṭa	ta ka di na	tom - ta -
a	b		a	b		c	d
tām - - ta	ki ṭa dī -	- ta ki ṭa	tām - - ta	ki ṭa dī -	- ta ki ṭa	ta ka di na	tom - ta -
a	a		a	a		c	d
tām - - ta	ki ṭa tām -	- ta ki ṭa	tām - - ta	ki ṭa tām -	- ta ki ṭa	ta ka di na	tom - ta -
a	b		a	b		c	d
tām - - ta	ki ṭa dī -	- ta ki ṭa	tām - - ta	ki ṭa dī -	- ta ki ṭa	ta ka di na	tom - ta -
a	a		d	a	b		c
tām - - ta	ki ṭa tām -	- ta ki ṭa	tom - ta -	tām - - ta	ki ṭa dī -	- ta ki ṭa	ta ka di na
a	a		d	a	b		c
tām - - ta	ki ṭa tām -	- ta ki ṭa	tom - ta -	tām - - ta	ki ṭa dī -	- ta ki ṭa	ta ka di na

11-149N
ending section: periya mōrā

ādi tāḷa

| • • • O • O •

a b

|di - - - |tān - gi ḍu |di ku ta ka |ta ri gi ḍu |ta - di - |tān - gi ḍu |di ku ta ka |ta ri gi ḍu

a c d c e

|di - - - |tān - gi ḍu |di ku ta ka |ta ri gi ḍu |ta lān - gu |tom - ta - |ta lān - gu |tōm - - -

a b

|di - - - |tān - gi ḍu |di ku ta ka |ta ri gi ḍu |ta - di - |tān - gi ḍu |di ku ta ka |ta ri gi ḍu

a c d

|di - - - |tān - gi ḍu |di ku ta ka |ta ri gi ḍu |ta lān - gu |tom - ta - |ta lān - gu |tōm - - -

a b

|di - - - |tān - gi ḍu |di ku ta ka |ta ri gi ḍu |ta - di - |tān - gi ḍu |di ku ta ka |ta ri gi ḍu

a c e b

|di - - - |tān - gi ḍu |di ku ta ka |ta ri gi ḍu |ta lān - gu |tōm - - - |ta - di - |tān - gi ḍu

c e a

|di ku ta ka |ta ri gi ḍu |ta lān - gu |tōm - - - |di - - - |tān - gi ḍu |di ku ta ka |ta ri gi ḍu

c d e c d e c d

|(ta lān - gu |tom - ta -) |[tōm - - -] |(ta lān - gu |tom - ta -) |[tōm - - -] |(ta lān - gu |tom - ta -)

11-150N
ending section: final kōrvai

ādi tāḷa

| • • • o • o •

khaṇḍa naḍai (five pulses per beat)

|ta - ta jem - |jem - ta ri ta |gu gu na ku ku |ta - di - - |gu gu na na ku |din - din - gu |di ku na ku ku |ta - di - -

|ta - ta jem - |jem - ta ri - |- - ta jem - |jem - ta ri - |ta - ta jem - |(ta di ki ṭa tom)|(ta di ki ṭa tom)|(ta di ki ṭa tom)

ABOUT THE AUTHOR

David Paul Nelson is an Artist-in-Residence in Music at Wesleyan University where he teaches South Indian percussion. He was the student of T. Ranganathan at the California Insitute of the Arts and at Wesleyan where he earned his Ph.D. in Ethnomusicology in 1991. He has accompanied top-ranked Karnatak musicians, including the late T. Viswanathan, in concerts around the world. Nelson maintains an active performance schedule in addition to teaching and writing about his subject.

VIDEO CREDITS

Introduction, examples, and solo performer: David Nelson

Tani for two players: Geoffrey Brown, David Nelson

Tani for four players: Ruby Ross, Aaron Paige, Dennis Chan, Geoffrey Brown

Video and post-production: Mariah E. Klaneski

Project Supervisor: Allynn Wilkinson